IF THESE WALLS COULD TALK

Other Books by Rachel

Essay

Parenthood: Has Anyone Seen My Sanity?
The Life-Changing Madness of Tidying Up After Children
This Life With Boys
Hills I'll Probably Lie Down On
We Count it All Joy

Poetry

this is how you know
Life: a definition of terms
The Book of Uncommon Hours
Textbook of an Ordinary Life
this is how you live

To see all the books Rachel has written, please click or visit the link below:
www.racheltoalson.com/writing

Rachel Toalson

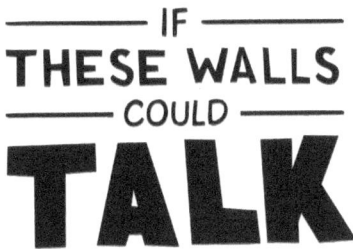

BATLEE
PRESS

Published by
Batlee Press
Post Office Box 591596
San Antonio, TX 78259

Copyright ©2019 by Rachel Toalson
All rights reserved.
Printed in the United States of America.
Interior design by Toalson Media.
Cover design by Ben Toalson. www.toalsonmarketing.com

No part of this book may be reproduced or transmitted in any form or by any means, electronic or mechanical, including photocopying and recording, or by any information storage and retrieval system, without permission in writing from the publisher. For information regarding permission, write to Batlee Press, PO Box 591596, San Antonio, TX 78259.

The author appreciates your taking the time to read her work. Please consider leaving a review wherever you bought it and telling your friends how much you enjoyed it. Both of those help get the book into the hands of new readers, which is incredibly important for authors. Thank you for your support.
www.racheltoalson.com

Names: Toalson, Rachel, author.
Title: If these walls could talk / Rachel Toalson
Description: First edition. | Batlee Press, Texas:
Batlee Press Books, 2019

10 9 8 7 6 5 4 3 2 1

First Edition—2019

To Ben, my partner in this laughter-filled journey.
May we always keep laughing,
no matter what the kids throw our way.
R.T.

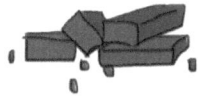

Contents

The Secrets We'll Never Tell (Okay, Maybe We Will)
3

True Confessions of an Exhausted Parent
49

The Parenting Life's a Big Mess
105

The Padded Walls of Parenthood
147

The Secret Life of Modern Parenting
179

Kids Make the World...Interesting
231

Foreword

The modern parenting world is a minefield of secrets, judgments, and unrealistic expectations that keep parents exhausted, full of fear, and eternally busy with trying to achieve some version of balance that may or may not exist. Many of us —myself included—are so caught up in the pursuit of being a good parent that there is rarely a moment when we don't feel the pressure of "someday" breathing down our backs. If we don't address this one little infraction because we don't have the energy to endure one more fight today, will he act entitled forever? If we have reached the end of ourselves and don't greet with compassion the one who fell off the trampoline and hurt his arm, will he be forever broken? If we take our eyes off of her for one second, will she be stolen, hurt, or worse?

We are "on" all the time. We are parenting in our separate circles, walling ourselves off because we're afraid that if "they," outside the walls of our home, take a peek inside, they will discover what we've feared since the day we became a parent: that we are not good enough—we are, in fact, terrible, reprehensible, lamentable parents. We fortify our walls to keep us safe. To keep our children safe.

Those walls are liars.

This book is my attempt to break down metaphorical walls

—both the ones that I have built myself in my years as a parent and the ones that the modern parenting world, with its never-ending list of expectations, has shoved into place. I have endeavored, through humor, to open up the walls of my home and provide a peek into the madness, frustration, and bliss that is, I think, a part of every parent's life.

At one time or another, every parent wonders if they are doing the right thing. Every parent longs for the occasional moments alone. Every parent delights in their kid one minute and can't wait for bedtime the next. If these walls could talk, they would say, *Yeah, me too.*

And isn't it good to know you're not alone?

As is usually the case with my humor essay books, these essays are not arranged in chronological order. You will read about my four-year-old twins in one essay and my five-year-old twins in another, and a couple pages later, those twins will be four again—not because I turned back time (I might elect to do that with some of my children, depending on the day, but almost certainly not these two), but because it made the most sense to me in the overall flow of the book. That "most sense" is subjective, of course, but suffice it to say that the age of the individual doesn't matter as much as the age of the "character" in the story. As it stands, my twins are now six and will have another birthday before this book publishes—because such is the nature of publishing.

I invite you to find a comfy chair, take a load off, and revel in walls that talk.

THE SECRETS
WE'LL NEVER TELL
(OKAY, MAYBE WE WILL)

The Grand Experiment that is Raising Children

I'm a working mom. I'm really good at what I do. I studied for four years in college and ended my time with a degree in journalism and English. I used to work as a managing editor for a newspaper, and I rocked that job every single day. Before that, I was a reporter. Now I'm an author.

I know exactly what I'm doing when faced with a blank screen. I know how to create stories from thin air, how to pull from my experiences and craft an essay that someone would actually want to read, how to position words on a page so that I can communicate what it is I'm trying to communicate in the most efficient (or entertaining) manner possible. I've been doing this every single day for more than a decade.

I've also been a mother every single day for almost a decade. You'd think that after this long, almost ten years spent in the School of Parenting, I would have a slight idea of what I'm doing.

I don't.

When I open the door to my twins' room, where they were supposed to be taking naps, and I see that they've just colored themselves green with a marker they smuggled into their room while their daddy's back was turned, I don't know what to do.

When the nine-year-old's mood flips at the drop of a LEGO mini figure and suddenly the whole entire world is ending, I don't know what I'm doing. When the normally complacent and obedient child becomes a back-talking fool and I have to address all that sass, I have no idea where to go from *What the —*.

 I study parenting books, poring over them for all the wisdom they have to offer me. I'll read examples about children in the middle of rebellion, and I'll think, "Yes, I can totally do this," and then the six-year-old will sneak out the door with a piece of gum I just told him he couldn't have and surreptitiously stick it in his mouth while his back is turned to me, and all of that wisdom dances right out the door with him.

 My children have the ability to turn me into a completely bumbling idiot with one disrespectful look or one ridiculous prank or one irreverent question or, well, simply their state of being.

 When they sneak out of their beds on a Saturday morning before the sun has even grinned its wake-up invitation, just so they can get into the frosted mini wheats and make sure they get their fair share, I don't know what I'm doing.

 When they eat half their brother's deodorant in the bathroom while everyone else is sleeping soundly in their beds, I don't know what I'm doing.

 When they fill up the bath water to a flooding point, even though they've been told a billion times not to do this, I don't know what I'm doing.

 When a boy comes home and tells me about being bullied

on his school playground, I don't know what I'm doing.

When the four-year-olds take the canister of gasoline that sits behind a locked shed door and pour it all over the yard, I don't know what I'm doing.

When they all wake up in a horrible mood, even though they got plenty of sleep (because I'm adamant about their sleep, since I'm adamant about my own), I don't know what I'm doing.

When they refuse to love each other, I don't know what I'm doing.

When the angry one threatens to run away because I'm the worst mom ever, I don't know what I'm doing.

When one wakes in the middle of the night just to tell me he's feeling sick and then, before the words are even completely out of his mouth, something else comes rocketing out of his mouth, too, I don't know what I'm doing.

When one of them is dealing with a flare-up of anxiety or depression, even though I've lived with these all my life, I don't know what I'm doing.

When one of them takes off his seatbelt in the car while we're driving seventy miles per hour down a busy highway, I don't know what I'm doing.

When I think of how impossible it is to give all of me to all of them, I don't know what I'm doing.

When they're all talking to me at the same exact moment in time, I don't know what I'm doing.

When they get into a slap-fight, I don't know what I'm doing.

When I tell them, no, they can't possibly fly from the top of their daddy's shed to the trampoline without breaking bones and they try it anyway (proving the "breaking bones" part wrong—which they'll remember, trust me), I don't know what I'm doing.

When the four-year-old cuts a huge hole in his brand new shirt, because someone left the scissors out in an accessible place, I don't know what I'm doing.

When I worry that I don't know how to help the one who flies off the handle, I don't know what I'm doing.

When I worry about them, period, I don't know what I'm doing.

When they mouth off one minute and then the next minute act like I'm their best friend, I don't know what I'm doing.

When I think about the next stage I'm coming into as a mother—the Puberty one—I don't know what I'm doing.

That's okay. Here's a secret many parents won't ever willingly tell you: We'll never completely know what we're doing. Our children are grand experiments—some days we get it right, some days we don't.

Before my twins were released from their twenty-day stay in the neonatal intensive care unit at our local hospital, Husband and I had to complete an infant CPR class in order to take them home. We learned all sorts of things we'd done wrong with our three older sons. At the end of the class, we looked at each other and sort of laugh-cried and agreed that it was a miracle they had all survived their first year.

It's a miracle *any* kid survives, because parents are all pretty much clueless.

We can spend a lifetime in this job and never feel quite competent at it. We can read books and take classes and listen to what other parents do and try it with our own, but the truth is, we're all basically on the same playing field—that is, amateurs. What works today probably won't work tomorrow. So just when we think we have it figured out, our kids will promptly show us that we don't actually have anything at all figured out.

Parenting is hard. We're dealing with some of the most irrational humans in existence—on an everyday, every-hour basis. We're never going to know everything. We'll never anticipate everything they'll do. We'll never be able to predict who our children will be when they wake up tomorrow. They are daily growing and changing and coming into their own bodies and minds, and that means the best we can do is sit back and let it happen and try to roll with the uppercuts, devising our next grand experiment for what might possibly work to shape them into rational, kind, courageous, creative, joyful, gracious, enjoyable adults.

No parent really knows what she (or he) is doing. That means we're all in good company.

Now, please excuse me, because my kid just told me I owe him a million dollars for making him sit down and do his homework and for being the worst parent in the history of the world, so I have an experiment that's calling my name.

Which is, of course, Mama.

Fantasies I Have While My Children are Talking

My house hears so many words. If these walls could talk, they would never, ever stop—because my kids never, ever stop, either.

I'm in the word business. I write for a living. I'm used to sorting through words all day, and I'm used to hearing a running commentary in my brain. But if one were to spend three minutes in my living room, one might think that being in the word business also means being in the listening-to-kids-talk-all-over-each-other business, because that's clearly what my kids believe. Someone is always talking. Someone else is always attempting to talk over that someone. And then someone else is trying, magnificently, to talk over the sum total of noise—two voices already yapping, the clatter of brothers playing, his daddy banging on the piano.

My system malfunctions every ten minutes.

Even though I'm in the word business, I use few of them to communicate verbally. This is likely a result of my journalism training. When I need to say something, I say it clearly and succinctly and leave it at that.

None of my kids inherited this trait. Every one of them inherited the communication style of Husband, which is a technique affectionately known as I Will Tell Sprawling Circular Stories and Release Rambling Thoughts at Random Because Words are Fun and the More the Merrier.

Which, I realize, is an excessively long way of saying Way Too Many Words. But alliteration. Go ahead. Read it again.

When one of the boys (or the man) in my house starts talking, I could catch the first couple of sentences, go out and mow the entire backyard, come back in and not have missed a thing, because everything in the middle was just "thinking out loud." All I need from them is the introduction and the conclusion, and I'm set. I know exactly what needs saying.

Now. This is not to say that I am not very, very glad that my kids enjoy talking to me, because the oldest is turning double-digits in November, and I know that the days of talking for hours are about to hit closing time (in more ways than one), and I'll be begging him to talk to me soon. So I always try my best to maintain the illusion of interest in my body language, keep focused eyes trained on their faces, and give the proper responses that let them know I'm listening (even if I'm not). This Fake Listening skill was also honed during my years spent in journalism, when I would conduct interviews with people who would tell me all about their nephew who'd been put in prison for embezzling the funds of his stepfather, rather than telling me about the hand-carved chess set they'd made for the International Chess Tournament, which was why I was there taking notes in the first place (I have one of those faces, I guess. And I'm also really good at listening. Or am I?).

But when my nine-year-old starts telling me about how he

traded this one Pokémon card to get another Pokémon card and how he's really glad that his friend had this one because he's been trying to find it for a while—and also he's decided to keep saving his money so he can buy a new package of Pokémon cards, maybe the fifteen-card pack, no, maybe he'll just go ahead and save up for the one-hundred-card pack, and these are all the things you should assess when you're considering a Pokémon card trade, and do you want to know how many Pokémon cards he has right now? my teeth start falling asleep.

This kid will hijack a whole afternoon if you mention the words "LEGO Minecraft" or "What do you want for your birthday" or "Poké—" (you can't even finish that one before he's off and running). He'll follow you around while you're changing the baby's diaper and while you're stirring soup on the stove and while you're pouring all the milk and setting the table, back and forth, back and forth, like an extra appendage I keep tripping over. He won't stop talking until all his brothers come crashing to the table and he can no longer hear himself over the voices vying for attention (we all give up on having any sort of conversation until everyone's shoveling food in their faces).

Get the seven-year-old started on talking about what he did in school today, and he'll tell you what he did and what all his classmates did, too, because he's the kind of kid who notices everything. You won't get a word in edgewise until you interrupt to ask him if he wants a fruit dessert tonight, okay, then, start eating dinner.

And then there's the five-year-old telling me about all the ways he could have killed himself today, because he's the daring one in the bunch who hangs upside down off the monkey bars and tries to leap over a fifteen-foot fence while bouncing on the trampoline. I'd rather not hear what he has to say.

My kids get better with practice. They're so skilled now at starting to talk about one thing and ending up on another subject entirely that I don't even feel bad about getting lost along the way anymore. It's anyone's guess how we got here.

Because one kid can use up to a billion words in one "quick" answer to a question, I've settled into a bit of a habit lately. I'm well aware that it's not a good habit. But it's one that keeps me sane, until we can figure out how to slow down the word vomit rocketing straight from their brains out their mouths.

When one of my kids opens his mouth and I know it will be a while before he closes it again, I find myself daydreaming.

My daydreams go a little something like this:

What would it be like to have a clean house?

I wonder if we could add house cleaning to our budget. Geez, I would have to clean the house before I even hired anyone to come clean it. That's embarrassing. Look at that sink. Disgusting. What kinds of animals live here? I don't even want to think about the bathrooms upstairs. Someone would come here and walk right back out, because it would be impossible to clean a house this dirty. They wouldn't be able to offer their money-back guarantee. It's probably too far gone for eco-friendly supplies, too. I wonder if any of my friends have a recommendation for a good house cleaning serv—

Oh, time for me to pay attention.

I wish it were the weekend.

I'm so glad Mom's taking the kids this weekend. It will be nice to sleep without six other bodies in the house. All these words. Sheesh. Are they ever done with words? Maybe I'll have some time to just lie on the bed and read without anybody wanting anything from me. Yeah, right. That's a lofty dream. I wonder what they'll do at Mom's. Probably play out in the dirt piles, which means I'll probably have to wash their shoes again, because they'll bring it all home. And the detoxing time. I forgot about the detoxing time. I'll have to add that into my schedule next week. It's always a pain getting them back into the routine. Well, I won't think about that right now. They'll be nightmares, but I'll be coming off a dream of a weekend.

"That sounds interesting," I say, once I notice a boy is finishing up.

I would like to go to bed now. Please?

I'm so tired. All these words make me more tired. I have a word limit, and I reached it half an hour after they got home from school. I need a break. What time is it? Five more hours. The bed is going to feel so nice. How long has he been talking? Twenty minutes? It can't be that long.

(At this point, my eyelids start drooping, and I require a pinch, which I fully recognize and execute efficiently enough to make my eyes water. My sons hardly ever notice their mama is almost crying during their story about how they did ninety-eight consecutive jumps over the jump rope in P.E. today—that's the gist, anyway. It's not anywhere close to that concise.)

We should learn sign language.

We really should. I bet that would keep my attention better, and, bonus, they wouldn't use so many words, because it would actually be work. This is a brilliant idea.

"I think we should learn sign language," I say, interrupting the five-year-old reading me an Elephant and Piggie book to demonstrate all the new words he knows now (he's been telling me about them for the last half hour).

Well, you know, this daydreaming while pretending to be listening isn't foolproof. I don't always get it right. But then I just invite in a lesson. "Remember how you interrupted Daddy when he was trying to talk to me earlier this morning? That's exactly how it feels."

Works every time.

What Freedom Means to Parents

One of my sons has a birthday four days after Independence Day. That was a delightful pregnancy here in South Texas, let me tell you. I begged Husband to let us move somewhere cooler that year: like maybe Antarctica. But my doctor said I couldn't travel to another continent when I was eight months pregnant, so, instead, I lounged indoors, where the air conditioner rattled to keep up, and poured my sweat all over the couch, hoping the sauna would somehow induce labor.

It didn't.

As we were nearing Independence Day this year, I thought about what it would be like to have a Parents' Independence Day, maybe once every year. I considered what freedom would mean to parents.

Husband and I get a little taste of this every now and then, when our parents take the kids for a weekend. So it's not an entirely foreign concept for us.

Here's what freedom typically looks like on a kid-less weekend:

Deciding to go somewhere, getting in the car, starting it, and pulling out of our driveway—all within a minute, start to finish.

Any time Husband or I have the (unsurprisingly) bad idea of packing up all the kids for a spontaneous outing—usually to the grocery store for something we (meaning I) forgot on the last trip—we have to give a warning of at least twenty minutes. Someone will misplace the shoes he had on two seconds ago; another someone will decide he needs to drop a load (and it's always the one who takes twenty minutes to accomplish this drop); another someone will slip on a banana peel his brother, in a moment of laziness, threw down on the driveway and face plant into the hood of the car, an injury for which he will need a giant Band-Aid across his face to stanch the bleeding (which isn't really that bad; he thinks it's worse than it actually is. Pshhh); another someone will play musical chairs with all the empty seats in the van instead of just getting into his own; and the last someone will realize he forgot to put on underwear— will he need underwear?

It doesn't matter if the grocery store is five minutes down the road and the trip will take a total of half an hour, there and back—leaving time will take at least triple that, if we're lucky.

Going to bed whenever you want.

I didn't appreciate this enough before I was a parent. I went to bed whenever I liked, and it did not even cross my mind that one day there might be a little someone waiting just outside my door, breathing underneath the crack because I locked it to keep them all out, trying to let me know that his brother stole his blanket and he doesn't want any of the four others that are already on his bed. I never imagined that I would see this child's hands wriggling under the door, as though to prove that, yes, he is real, and, yes, he needs his blanket back. I had not a clue that bedtime—mine, at least—was such a gift.

No amount of ignoring this almost-intruder will make him go away. I'll go to bed when he lets me, I guess.

Sleeping in on the weekends.

Even though, when my sons are in school, they rarely get right out of bed when I wake them up at 6:30 a.m., during the summer and on weekends, they're sure to be up by 5:45 at the latest. I try to pretend I don't hear the noise of feet. But anxiety usually drags me from my bed, whether I like it or not; boys are not safe alone—at least not yet. I know what happens when my sons are unaccompanied for any amount of time. Someone will try to fly with a kite strapped to himself (even though he saw his brother get mangled yesterday for the same thing) or challenge his brother to a duel with steak knives ("just don't really cut each other." Yeah, that's gonna help) or pour himself a giant bowl of raw oats with milk and then leave it for the flies, because, go figure, he doesn't really like it.

A perfectly tidy house.

This one made the list for other people. I doubt my house will ever be perfectly tidy, even when the kids are gone. I have a Husband, after all. And also a me. I've been known to put a book down somewhere and lose it in the stacks that follow me everywhere.

Eating in peace, while it's hot.

It never fails. I bring out some leftovers from the date night with Husband, and the kids are immediately circling me like scavengers. "Can I have a bite?" they'll say.

"No," I'll say.

"Why not?" they'll say, their faces falling into the saddest pouts ever.

"Because this is my food," I'll say.

"You're mean," they'll say.

"That's right. I am," I'll say, because I'll do whatever it takes to eat my ziti al forno in peace. I deserve this.

Cooking for two.

I don't even remember what this looks like. That's probably why, when Husband and I send the kids off for a weekend, we mostly eat out. Because how do you cook for two when you're used to cooking for a small army?

Silence.

I love silence. I love sitting in a room and hearing nothing but my own thoughts. It doesn't happen often, because someone at my house is always talking. I get to the end of a day with my sons and there are so many words stuffed up in my head that I feel like I might explode.

Just the other day, I told my nine-year-old that I was on word overload and needed a few minutes of quiet, and he said, "Well, you haven't exploded yet" and kept right on talking about the next stop motion movie he's going to make—which is super cool, but words. So many words.

I know these freedoms seem somewhat wonderful and exotic when you're living the day in, day out life of a haggard parent, but, truthfully, by the time a weekend without my sons ends, I'm ready to get them all back, because there's something about silence and easy road trips and eating in peace that feels a little eerie now. I'm glad for the madness that kids bring to my life, because it's not the *freedom* that matters so much as the *living*. And my sons show me how to live every moment of every day—by "accidentally" throwing dodge balls at my face and sneaking bites of my date-night leftovers when I get up to pour myself some water and gathering the wildflowers in the front yard, which they'll try to put in my hair, dirty roots and all.

My sons have shown me how to play, how to dream, how to love. They have freed me in a million ways.

So my Independence Day? It happened when I had kids.

10 Movie Titles that Describe the Lives of Parents

The other day Husband and I were out on the town, with the children, and a succession of things went wrong. One kid tripped and fell, another kid climbed into the bottom of the grocery cart against the advice of his father and pinched his finger, and a third one ran into a glass door. It took us twenty minutes to get from the parking lot to the inside of the store.

Every now and then I feel like I'm in the middle of a bad movie. Without all the glamor. Infused with a whole lot of satire.

Here are some movies that could tell the story of my life as a mom.

Gone with the Wind

Tagline: What is she feeding them?

Featuring a mom who tries desperately to get away from her kids' farts, because she's almost lost her entire olfactory sense in the cheek trumpet concerts that have graced her house in recent days, this movie follows the main character, named Mama, as she races through every room in her house, trying to open every door, while the noxious gas, depicted by a visible thick chartreuse cloud, slowly stink bombs the set. She discovers, tragically, that she is locked inside her house with the killer scent, and, in the end, she passes out for lack of clean air and oxygen. Her sons stand in a circle around her prone body, laughing hysterically about the wonder of their anatomies, which, of course, releases more pops and frats (stet) from the fanny flappers. They can't get over the fact that they *do* have a super power for long enough to help Mama up. And, unfortunately, the noxious gas cloud is still alive. They collapse on the floor around her, betrayed by their own bodies.

The Phantom Menace

Tagline: Now you see me, now you don't

This movie stars two identical twins who can weave in and out of invisibility, much as they do in real life. They're so good on their feet that they send a mother and father on a wild chase to figure out what they're doing before they do it—but, of course, the parents are always one step behind as the twins unclog a toilet with a plunger that sloshes brown water everywhere, dump over a container of kitty litter so they can examine all the poop lumps buried within it, and disappear at the city zoo and then magically reappear half an hour later, when a zoo employee finds them climbing up the walls of the crocodile exhibit.

The Lion King

Tagline: Ever heard a roar this loud?

This film features a kid who's trying his hardest to put together an amazing LEGO creation. Unfortunately, his little brothers keep messing him up. By talking. He says they're being way too loud and breaking his concentration, but when everything is so quiet you could hear a pin drop, he still fails to put those LEGO pieces together to his satisfaction. And then the climax: a roar so loud it breaks every window in his house.

E.T. The Extraterrestrial
Tagline: Are you ready for the perfect storm?

Featuring six boys who are like aliens to their mother, this is the story of the difference between boys and a woman. She doesn't understand what they're trying to do half the time, and she doesn't know if she even wants to understand something as crazy as this. Every time she asks them why they do what they do, they shrug and say, "I don't know." Though slow of plot, this movie is not slow of humor, as boys attempt to roller blade down stairs, do skateboard tricks on a trampoline, and see who can elicit the loudest face-smack when he runs into the backyard fence.

The Hunger Games
Tagline: Think you have enough food? You don't.

This movie features a series of family dinners in which the actual cooked and/or prepared food becomes more and more plentiful. But during each family dinner the kids continuously complain that they're still hungry and there's nothing left to feed them. They raid the refrigerator at all hours of every day, and, on grocery shopping day, they have a fight to the near-death to see who will choose from the new food first. Throughout the movie, you'll see the games this family plays at dinner (which do little to distract starving boys), the unbelievable (and interminable) snacks and table feasts, and what boys will do to get extra food before their brothers.

The Jungle Book

Tagline: Wild monkeys only need imaginary trees

This movie follows the journey of one monkey through the wild jungles of home. Watch as he maneuvers flushing the toilet (when he hasn't actually used it), turning off lights (which he hardly ever does), and cleaning his room (which certainly looks like a jungle). Watch as he attempts to do homework and practice the piano and tell a story about his day in the middle of the jungle. Watch as he outruns those who would like to trip him up at every turn and finally finds his way to the ultimate payoff: food.

Transformers

Tagline: Ask me again. I've changed my mind.

This movie features humorous scenes in which indecisive children pick out their clothes, pack their own school lunches, and go about doing activities throughout the day. One minute they will want to go to the pool so badly they could cry, and the next minute they're complaining because their trip to the pool means they didn't get to watch a movie tonight. It's like trying to keep up with a sugar-overdosed hummingbird that changes directions every other second. Also features a short sequence of scenes in which a child acts kind, compliant, and helpful and a follow-up scene in which the same kid acts like a holy terror.

Monsters, Inc.

Tagline: What's this creature in my house?

This movie features a day in the life of two parents who get their kids home from a weekend visit with the grandparents. It will be filled aplenty with tantrums, screams, complaints about dinner, and constant explosions on the floors of every room in the house as the children show their parents everything the grandparents gave them to bring home. The children will also battle their parents on things like taking a bath, coloring on paper instead of walls, and, of course, going to bed. At the end of this humor tale, a closeup of two frazzled parents collapsing into bed will provide the perfect resolution for this less-than-perfect day.

I am Legend

Tagline: Last man standing wins

This tale stars a strong-willed ten-year-old in the role of Legend and pits parent against child in an ultimate battle of wills: How many times can he ask for something (in different ways) before his dad will cave? How many whys and why nots will he be permitted before his mom starts to wear her crazy eyes? How many words will he spout before a surrender flag lifts in the background? In addition to his constant arguments, this child will be followed around as he never stops talking. The film features interesting camera angles, four hundred hours of bloopers (monologues), and a compelling look at what it takes to break a parent.

Skyfall

Tagline: They're both a train wreck and a plane crash

Starring the harried parents of young children, this movie follows them throughout their day-to-day operations—getting kids off to school, working, coming home, fighting through homework, preparing dinner, and, finally, wrestling kids into bed. These parents put on a good show, but what's it really like inside the confines of their home? They can't get it together—see all those newspapers stacking up on the counter? They haven't read them in a month. And the kids add more school papers to the towering stack. Will they ever get a handle on things? Probably not.

So I play a starring role in at least one of these films practically every day of the year. At least I get paid a movie star salary.

Wait. I think I got the short end of this stick.

Along Came a Spider: a Tale of Mild Disappointment

I had just picked up my sons from school, and we were trying to get everybody loaded in the car. I was in the middle of strapping the baby in his seat, when my second son, who stood behind me, made an innocent observation: "Mama, there's a spider on you."

For you to fully understand the significance and weight of this innocent observation, I must tell you that I am the daughter of a woman who used to beat spiders to death with a broom when she found them crawling anywhere—all while shrieking hysterically. I am a woman whose son once dropped a spider on my lap because he picked it up and thought it was cool, and I ran away screaming in the middle of a worship set at church. I am also a woman who has had a spider drop into my lap while I'm driving, and I nearly drove off a cliff.

So when my son said this, I immediately felt the fear make my legs grow warm and soft. Heat rushed over my chest.

"Get it off," I said rather calmly. I was quite proud of my calm.

My son merely stood there looking at my back, so I thought maybe he was kidding. Boys are pranksters, after all. I shook my head, tried to still my fluttering heart, and said, "You shouldn't joke like that."

My third son, who was already in the back seat of our van, leaned over at that moment to look. "Oh, my goodness," he said. "It's white. It's almost in your hair."

Something about the way he said it told me he wasn't kidding. This was not a joke.

It was not my finest moment. Imagine, if you will, a woman flailing in the middle of a sidewalk near an elementary school, trying desperately to swat the spider off her back—and then add about twenty percent more hilarity and ridiculousness. That was me. I finally slammed my back up against my van, bruised my shoulder blades, and finished off the spider—or so I hoped. My sons couldn't tell me one way or another, and I felt it crawling up the back of my neck all the way home.

Husband checked to see if it was gone when I walked in the house. He didn't see anything, and I'm hoping that's enough.

Some people, when they see me out and about with all my sons, will occasionally say something to the effect of "You're a lucky mom to have all these boys protecting you." This is usually when I'm walking into Target with Batman, Spider-Man, and Yoda beside me because they didn't want to take off their costumes and I didn't have the energy for a fight. But you get used to hearing things like that when you're the mom of boys.

The problem, however, is that my sons are just as afraid of creepy crawly things as I am. They see a bug they can't identify, and they high-tail it out of there. A scorpion moves toward them on the floor, and, rather than smash it with the shoe that's on their foot, they skedaddle. A bee once chased one of them, and he nearly ran through a wall trying to get away.

When you become the mom of a son, you imagine your sons standing by your side, swatting away things like spiders and scorpions and bees without even batting an eye. These are the boys who forget to drain the tub and leave the toilet seat up and don't want to hang up their clothes. This protection is supposed to make all that worth it. I'm not supposed to even think about insects or arachnids or whatever might come crawling my way.

When we got home, there was another spider on the floor, large and black and heading straight for the ten-year-old's stinky feet (though I can't fathom why). He refused to kill it, saying it needed to be relocated—and yet, when we all wondered aloud who might do the relocating, he pointed right at me.

We argued about it until we looked again and the spider was gone.

The worst kind of spider, in my opinion, is the one you know is there but can't see.

Random Places I've Found Library Books: a Modern Mystery

If you know me and my family at all, you know that one thing we love to do is read together. We read before nap time, when one of the three-year-old twins will pick out two picture books and I'll read a few chapters from the middle grade novel we're currently consuming (our pick this week is *Echo*, by Pam Muñoz Ryan). We read audiobooks while doing chores, when we don't feel like listening to the kids complain about our '90s retro station and how it "really is hurting our ears because this is the worst music ever. Seriously. Minecraft music is so much better."

That's a direct quote.

We'll read during bath time and laugh about Shel Silverstein's bizarre poetry—at least until my sons tell me I'm not allowed inside the bathroom because they're getting too big and want their privacy. And we read before bed.

The kids and I head out to our local library at least once a week, because libraries are magical places for children. Some of my fondest memories as a kid are the ones where my mother set us loose in the local library and told us to pick out enough books to last us a week, which, of course, meant I needed at least twenty.

I love libraries so much that I set one up in my own home. My six sons share two bedrooms, but we have a library, because priorities.

All those trips to our public library are not without, inevitably, lost books.

There are so many things that never happened before I had kids. Bouncing a check (I can't even add correctly anymore). Leaving something important at a store (I'll leave my checkbook in the basket, but at least I have all my kids). Paying a library fine.

I'm convinced that we are some of the biggest supporters of the San Antonio Public Library system, which is all well and good, except that when I pay for a book, I'd like to keep it. Instead, library books that are fortunate enough to come home with my kids fall into a giant black hole that is my sons' bedrooms.

I'm being modest, actually. The entire house is marked as a black hole. (This is why we lose socks, shoes, homework, permission slips, underwear, and food. This black hole really likes food.)

Sometimes we never find these library books. Sometimes they show up in the most unlikely (or most obvious) of places. Like:

The car

This one's not so hard to believe. We do, after all, drive to the library, and my sons can't wait to get home to read their library books—they get a head start in the car. That drive home is the quietest drive Lucy, our van, witnesses each week; I really need to think of a way to utilize this to my advantage. Usually, I just marvel at the miraculous silence while glancing at them every now and again in the rearview mirror, to make sure they're still breathing.

Once we get home, though, they are visually reminded of what they were doing before we packed up to visit the library—dumping out all the LEGO pieces we own, pretending the front and back doors are revolving doors, dressing up as Spider-Man, no Iron Man, no maybe a SWAT team member with red silk gloves and a Robin Hood hat. So they race out of the van, their books long forgotten. Those books will be trampled the next time we load up, but, hey, at least they'll have something to do for the five-minute trip to the store. Win.

Husband and I do search the car, of course. But by the time we get around to it, the forgotten library books are now covered in a layer of paper airplanes, discarded drawings, and clothes they...well, I don't know, didn't want to wear? The minds of boys are hard to follow.

That layer must be removed before library books can be found. And who has energy for that?

The laundry hamper

Maybe they were reading a book in the bathroom when they took off their clothes, and, because they were finished with it, they weren't all that bothered when the book got tangled up in their sleeves, and then, because kids aren't all that observant, they didn't notice the hard corners sticking out when they actually put their clothes in the hamper.

Like they put their clothes in the hamper. It was probably

me. And I'm always in such a hurry to be out of their swampy bathroom, I don't pay attention to anything that might be hanging out in the pile of clothes.

I probably should, though, because now I feel compelled to replace these Pokémon Ruby & Sapphire books for the simple fact that they smell like wet dog and rotten Fritos.

In the trash can

This is most likely the work of the three-year-old twins. They are, you see, some of the most efficient instigators in my house. If a brother says he really likes the song pounding through the speakers, the three-year-old will sneak up to the iPhone and turn it off. If a brother says, "Please stop copying me," a three-year-old will do exactly the opposite. For hours. If a brother says he really likes this book he's reading and he happens to leave that book unattended for half a second, well, there it goes in a container with last night's chicken bones, somebody's old toast with jam, and their baby brother's fully loaded diaper.

And we never even think to look, because who would?

In the refrigerator

Book preservation? A book and a snack? Someone mistook the fridge shelf for a bookshelf? Your guess is as good as mine.

I suppose if library fines are the price I have to pay for kids who will read to stave off boredom, then I'll take it.

Besides, now that they make an allowance, it's my sons' responsibility to pay for their lost library books.

And they've suddenly become much more attentive. Wish

I'd known that trick years ago. I could have saved [redacted] dollars.

(Trust me, you don't want to know.)

On the Circus of Leaving When You're a Parent

Ever wonder why parents are practically late to everything?

I could tell you a million stories of the mishaps that slink in while we're looking the other way (toward the destination: the minivan)—spilled milk, accidental excrement, shirts showing up with holes that no one cut out with scissors, they promise. But these stories would likely take all day.

Instead, I'm going to share a little known look at what most often gets parents from *we're actually on time for once* to *Now we're half an hour late. We shouldn't have said anything.*

The Secret Life of a Kid

Your dad says the magic words: "Time to get in the car!" But you know you actually have about ten minutes to play around before he has his coffee ready and your mom finishes making sure everyone has used the potty. So that's exactly what you're going to do: play around. With LEGO pieces, with stuffed animals, maybe even with your brother's shoes.

You always seem to forget that it's going to take you at least half an hour to put on your shoes—most of that time spent looking for those shoes. What can you say? Remembering is not your strongpoint.

But that's okay. You have, with practice, composed a handy step-by-step guide for putting on your shoes. It goes like this:

1. When your dad says you better find your shoes, walk around. It's important that you walk around, because your parents won't help you find your missing shoes if they don't think you're making an effort.

2. Announce you can't find your shoes. Do this in a semi-calm voice—because you know that whining sets them on edge and you're not looking for the edge. Yet. Whining will come in handy later, to successfully escalate the situation. It's true that you haven't really looked for these missing shoes, but your parents don't have to know that.

3. Wait for your mom or dad to help you find your shoes. Sometimes you'll be waiting a while, because they think you're old enough now to search on your own (have they seen your room?). But that's too much work. Sooner or later they'll be so desperate to leave the house that they'll come running to help you find your shoes. Or they'll simply get tired of hearing your singsong, "I can't find my shoes."

4. Now that your parents have found your shoes, sit down to put them on. You really intend to put them on. It's just that your brother is there, building something with his LEGO pieces, and it's not fair. Why does he get to play while you're stuck putting on shoes?

5. Allow yourself to get distracted by what your brother's doing. That thing he's working on—you're not really sure what it is, but you can already see where improvements could be made—is pretty cool. As you draw closer to him, you see your

other brother reading. That cover on the book looks amazing! That book is probably one you want to read, too. So you do. Over his shoulder.

6. Effectively lose your shoes again. It's not your fault. Somebody moved them.

7. Complain that you've probably lost your shoes forever, because they're not anywhere. You know—you looked this time. They're not anywhere. How could they disappear? You don't know. This is weird.

8. Laugh when your dad points at your shoes, which are practically right in front of your face, because he just did the most amazing magic trick. He made your shoes appear from thin air!

9. Put on your left shoe.

10. Oops. You forgot to go potty, and you now have to go so badly you can't hold it, so leave the other shoe where it is and walk one-shoed to the bathroom. Your mom will be glad you're doing this before you get into the car.

11. Forget to flush. That goes without saying.

12. Return to the place where you left your right shoe, and bemoan the fact that it is missing. Again.

13. Trip over the right shoe on your way out the door so you can tell your dad you lost your shoes again.

14. Remember that you forgot to put socks on, and you know your mom doesn't like it when you wear shoes without socks, so take off the left shoe you already put on and made the effort to tie, and leave it beside your right shoe, which you found after you tripped over it. Funny.

15. Go upstairs for some socks. Complain that there aren't any clean.

16. Argue with your mom about how you're supposed to be doing your own laundry now (when did you have time?! You were too busy being bored all week!).

17. Get distracted by something your dad is saying—did he just tell your mom you're going to eat pizza today? Insert yourself into this much more interesting conversation.

18. Return to your shoes, which are, surprise, surprise, missing yet again.

19. Ask your dad to help you find them. Put plenty of whine in the tone this time. This is urgent. Someone stole your shoes!

20. Put on the shoes your dad found. Try to tie them. Your fingers hurt, though, from all this searching for shoes. Seriously. You think maybe they're broken and you'll never be able to tie your shoes again.

21. Make a screeching noise every time the laces wrap around your hurting fingers. This will usually work in your favor after a minute or so. But your dad isn't paying attention yet. Keep trying. Screeching, that is.

22. Oh, well. You're fast on your feet. Untied laces won't trip you up, so race out to the van. At least you're not a rotten egg. Your dad is still standing in the doorway with his hands on his hips.

It's been three hours since your dad said it was time to leave, and your mom will cry she's so happy to finally be close to leaving. And while you're looking at her, you'll trip yourself on your untied shoelaces and scrape your nose on the slide toward the car, for which you'll need a Band-Aid. And probably a change of clothes. You've never liked the fashion known as Asphalt Dirt with a side of Sidewalk Chalk.

You probably should have just stayed home.

Welcome to Minecraft Motherhood: a Half-Hearted Celebration

He's following me around, trying to tell me about what he did in Minecraft today, as if I care.

I want to care. Of course I do. Minecraft is important to him. I want to care about the things that are important to him. It's just that it's 4:30, and I'm trying to cook, and he's following me around like a shadow, talking. Incessantly talking. About Minecraft.

The water is boiling over, because I keep tripping over him on my quest to reach it and turn down the heat. The back door is open, because someone ran out and neglected to remember they weren't born in a stable (though the house smells like one). The twins have noticed that Mama is otherwise engaged —and, unfortunately, not just with dinner. That's an easy one. I can still hear what they're doing when I'm focusing on the preparation of dinner. But when there is an endless drone in my ear, reciting every part of his Minecraft adventure today? A few things slip through the cracks. Right now, they're cutting their shirts into tiny little pieces while I crack the spaghetti in half, drop it in the boiling water, and try not to poke my drone in the eye.

Welcome to Minecraft Motherhood.

If These Walls Could Talk

This boy has always had a lot to say. He started talking when he was two because he didn't want to waste any time. Back then he talked about simple things—what he was reading in science books (which was always interesting to me), expounding on metaphors when he felt angry ("These are my missiles!" as he pointed at his arms), and offering unique and creative observations about the world around him ("This tree bark looks like your belly." Thanks, kid.).

Now he has entered a stage I've heard is pretty typical for boys his age: Minecraft. We don't allow him to play often, just for a window of time—half an hour—every day if he so chooses. He always chooses. He also always chooses to talk about Minecraft for about five times as long as he gets to play it.

I try to listen. I really do. I tell myself that if I don't listen to these seemingly small things, he will not trust me to listen to the large things. It's just that I've never been interested at all in video games. When my brother would spend hours in front of the Nintendo back when we were kids, I chose to pull out my mother's volumes of Emily Dickinson poetry and Shakespeare masterpieces (what can I say? I was an interesting kid).

So, inevitably, when my son talks nonstop about Minecraft for four hours, my eyes glaze over a bit. I'm way, way out of my league, even though I spent years as a reporter and you'd be surprised by the long tangents people will take when a reporter stands in front of them.

Most of the time I have no idea what he's talking about, so I play along. He's so excited. I try to follow suit and act excited, too. I fail just about every time.

I want my son to know that he is heard, that I love him and that he can talk to me about anything. Ideally, I'd like that "anything" to be something more like friends or school concerns or his anxiety or his budding interest in girls (no, not really—not yet). I would rather not listen to twelve thousand words of uninterrupted Minecraft talk. If I'm not careful, I can begin to think that the only thing he cares about is Minecraft. But that's not true. He cares about other things—his brothers, his health, me ("I'll get you a Shel Silverstein poetry book for your birthday Mama," he said the other day—the first break in Minecraft-speak in three hours).

Even if it's not ideally what I want to hear about, at least he's talking. And because I want to make sure that line of communication always stays open, I pretend to listen, ask questions every now and then, and smile when I think he's finished (he never really is—the smile only encourages him to say more).

Meanwhile, the twins have now taken the scissors to their brother's homework—and quite deftly, I might add.

Ah, well. At least the house isn't burning down around us…yet.

A Realistic Look at Having a Large Family

Having a large family is a challenging endeavor—and not only for the reasons you'd think. Of course there are the logistics of things—where to put kids, how to feed them, what to do about baths. There are the emotional things—checking in with them when their hearts are hurting, assessing the anger that's bursting out of them more often lately, keeping tabs on time spent with each.

There are also the challenges that relate to other people. When you have a large family, people will call you selfish, tell you you're ridiculous for procreating so many times, crack crude jokes about keeping your hands off each other (it's very hard. Husband is hot, and I'm not so bad myself.).

I don't care about these insults all that much. Mostly I think people should mind their own business. Sometimes they really get to me, and those are the days I have to take stock of my situation and see it for what it is.

When I get down in the dumps about how hard it is, on multiple levels, to have so many children, I remember that (a) it was my choice, and (b) there are many pros to it as well. Here's a look at some of the pros and cons of having a large family.

Pro: You have an excuse for everything.

You can be late anywhere, because all you have to do is say that one of your kids was not cooperating with the instructions Get In the Car Right Now and made it impossibly difficult to leave the house. And people will believe you, because, yeah, kids are bad at leaving the house (and a lot of other things, too).

You can also use your kids as an excuse for not volunteering (Oh, my son is sick), not going somewhere (We just got rid of lice), or not joining the PTA (I have too many kids). You can use your kids as your excuse for not keeping up with things—they are the reason you don't sign school folders (there are too many folders), the reason you filed your story late (they completely deleted it from your computer; true story!), the reason you never get out and do anything anymore (it's so much work!), and the reason you can't accomplish anything great and significant in your life (whatever helps you feel better).

Con: All those excuses are mostly true.

You won't be able to keep up with the folders, you won't be able to keep up with work (at least when you work from home), you won't be able to do much of anything to your original standards. You won't be able to stay on top of the dishes or laundry or constant food preparation, and you'll have to hire a cleaning service just to make sure your home remains livable, because you certainly don't have time to clean the house when your kids are running through the kitchen with a pair of knives they'll use to turn a box into a stuffed animal hotel or shoving three pounds of grapes in their kissers or playing with the candle-lighter. You don't even remember your name half the time, your head is spinning so fast.

Pro: You get to drive a minivan.

Minivans are the best. So much storage, so much comfort, and pretty good gas mileage for the size of the vehicle.

Con: That minivan is crammed, and it smells bad.

When we originally bought Lucy, our Honda Odyssey, ten years ago, we thought we'd never ever ever let the kids eat in the car. We would keep everything nice and clean and orderly. Now we're doing well to drop them off in the school drop-off line without losing an important paper among the stacks of them filling the car. And every time you open the door (which the safety guards have to do at the elementary school, because our minivan is prehistoric and doesn't have automatic-open doors), you get a whiff of fart, old cheese, and soured milk. Sometimes I want to cry over that soured milk.

Pro: There are a lot of hands to help.

This can be a definite pro if they're actually helping. If they're not, see below.

Con: There are also a lot of hands to destroy.

My kids are everywhere. Just when I've told one of them not to do something, another is trying to do the exact same thing, because apparently rules only apply to individuals, not the wholes. And it's going to take a raised voice—which I don't like using—to stop them from doing it, even though they already know. It's just so much fun to try.

There are hands everywhere—in the cookies I baked this

morning, in the art cabinet I always feel foolish filling, in the books that never make it back on shelves, in last night's pizza dinner, in their pants.

Pro: I've never laughed so hard in my life.

Kids are hilarious. Not a day passes that I don't find myself laughing almost until I cry. This is an easy benchmark for me; when I'm tickled to death, I can't help but cry. I get so much humor material from my sons I'm going to be out of a job when they grow up and leave.

Con: I've never spent so much money in my life.

When "they" say kids are expensive, "they" know what they're talking about. Kids are incredibly expensive. I have never spent so much money on food, clothes, allowances, and everything in between. They lose library books, they put holes in walls, they accidentally tear up important things. They leave lights on, forget to flush, peel paint, and do a thousand other things that cost money besides just food, shelter, and clothing.

Pro: You make people uncomfortable.

When I go to any family or friend get-together, people are always cracking jokes about our large family (it makes them uncomfortable to see so many well-behaved boys in one place, I think). When we descend upon the public, people stare. When I write about my family, I can always count on nasty comments, offensive emails, and sometimes, for the ones who are really dedicated, hate mail in the actual mailbox. It's great.

I don't care about making people uncomfortable. I've gotten used to the snarky comments. We know who we are, and it's not usually who they assume we are.

Con: You make people uncomfortable.

It's been a while since Husband and I have hung out with friends. It's hard to get together with people when you have so many children who need supervision at pretty much all times. It's not an easy thing to be part of groups as a family or join in celebrations as a family or do anything spontaneous as a family. You don't always feel welcome when you're going places—more like an inconvenience, actually. I'm not complaining; I'm being honest. It is what it is, and we have to deal with that.

But even though most days I find myself leaning more toward the difficult pieces of having a large family, it's been one of the best things in my life. I'm glad we decided to have six children. It has its own advantages—and the advantage of such brilliant, effusive, loyal love is among its greatest. There is enough love in our home to change the world—and that's exactly what we plan to do.

Watch out, world. Here we come.

TRUE CONFESSIONS OF AN EXHAUSTED PARENT

The Laughable Illusion of 'I Have it All Together'

One early morning last spring, after I dropped off my three older sons at their school down the road from our house and was walking the younger three back home, a woman pulled up beside us and rolled down the window of her truck.

I don't know what my face looked like; it's a little disconcerting when someone pulls up beside you in a vehicle while you're walking, and, also, I have an overactive imagination. My thoughts in those moments were most definitely the worst. I braced myself to bolt, mentally running through a haphazard survival strategy whereby I would plant my twins on my lower legs for a "ride" and run for dear life with the baby strapped in the stroller.

I opened my mouth to scream.

But the person parked beside me was just the mom of another kindergartener at school. And all she wanted to say was, "I see you every morning walking your sons to school, and you look so calm and collected. You just, I don't know, seem like you have it all together."

I almost laughed. Hysterically. But, thinking better of this situationally inappropriate response, I instead said, "Thank you. I guess I put on a good show." Which must have taken her off guard a little, because she gave a nervous laugh, waved, rolled up her window, and sped away.

I don't try to put on a show. I try to be very transparent about how unarguably hard it is to mother six sons. But we never know what happens behind closed doors, and my doors are often closed (usually because boys are only half-dressed—or not dressed at all). So I want to make a public announcement: I don't have it all together. Not even close. Not even a little bit close. Not even—

You get the picture.

Just this morning, I yelled at my kids because one of them was picking a booger out of the other's nose and then sticking his hands in his oatmeal to eat [gag], rather than using the spoon I'd put beside his bowl. Last night, after I'd folded the laundry all nice and neat, someone unfolded it by taking a running leap right into the middle of it while we were supposed to be having a family dance party. We found ourselves in the middle of an unexpected underwear explosion (at least it was the clean kind), and I just about lost my mind (but did not explode my underwear). Yesterday afternoon, my twins dismantled their ceiling fan during their "nap" so when I went to "wake them up," it was hanging by four wires—and I'll admit it: I had six handfuls of chocolate chips before I remembered that we'd done a Lifestyle Change and chocolate chips are not included in that (why are they around, then?).

During the school year, Husband and I are the Worst Parents Ever. I don't sign any of the folders or papers; there are too many—and I'm speaking in terms of papers *and* children. I hardly even have time to look at all the papers they bring home; they usually sit in a leaning tower until I summon the energy at the end of the week to move them from the counter to the recycling bin, because it's now too late to sign any of them (purposeful or accidental? I'll never tell.). My sons' teachers have had to track me down for field trip permission slips and reminders about special projects and important dates. (I'm sorry, teachers. Truly. It's hard to care about signing papers when your four-year-olds won't stay out of the un-flushed toilet while you're "distracted" trying to make tomorrow's school lunches.)

The sheets in our house haven't been washed in [redacted], because the thought of stripping the beds and then making them up again is intimidating in a house with eight loads of weekly laundry and six beds (not counting mine) that would need stripping and remaking. The toilets? Well, we'll just say it's about time to invest in some new ones, because boys and toilets are frenemies. The walls are scuffed and chipped and colored with crayons, because there are six clowns in my house, and they're all the ringmaster of their own individual circus. (Yes. Clowns can be ringmasters, too.)

Most days I let my sons dress themselves because I'm too exhausted to care, and, also, I don't relish fighting with a four-year-old who doesn't know the definition of "clean" about whether he can wear the same shirt he had on yesterday, even though it smells like saturated monkey fur. I just hide it and look the other way when my sons step out of the house looking more like a pauper's closet blew up than the cool kids I know they are. Their knees flap through holes in their sweatpants, someone went through a chewing-the-collar stage and now his brothers look like they're doing the same, and half of them have mismatched shoes. With no socks, likely. I don't care. There's always our yearly family pictures in which to project the image that we have it all together and are not actually rowing a boat gently down the stream with six merrily gaping holes in it.

Life is a dream.

I used paper plates for my sons' lunch yesterday, which isn't, in itself, bad (we don't use them often; global warming is a concern in our house), but when I went to grab a couple from the top of the washing machine, my hand knocked over a glass mason jar, which also wouldn't have been all that bad except.

Except the entire morning had been one clean-up session after another. Someone dropped his bowl of cinnamon spice oatmeal, someone else tried to take a gallon of milk out of the refrigerator and didn't know the lid wasn't completely secured, someone else accidentally pushed over his mug of tea because he was horsing around with the only brother left at the table.

I sat down and cried.

Because I have it all together.

When one of my sons threw a LEGO piece and hit another one right in the center of the forehead, I just about did the same to him—because I get so tired of all the fighting, and I really can't stand it when they hurt one another. They're supposed to be best friends.

When one decided to turn a forward flip off his top bunk and hurt himself in the process, I shrugged my shoulders and said, "That's what happens when you don't listen"—because he's been told a billion times not to try it, and I'm an empathic parent.

One of them shredded his curtains during nap time, because he smuggled into his room a surprisingly dull wall decoration and stashed it behind his bottom bunk and then waited until I'd closed the door to take it out and start destroying—silently, of course.

The only thing I did halfway right today was kiss my kids goodnight, even though I didn't really want to, after the ringer they'd put me through. All I really wanted to do was go to bed and close my eyes and start all over again tomorrow.

Hopefully getting my act together. (We're hard on ourselves, aren't we?)

Maybe it seems like I have it all together because people can't really imagine my reality—and my sons *are* pretty remarkable. But I assure you, I am just as flawed as every other parent out there. My children are just as flawed as every other kid alive today.

Trust me. They're all supposed to be sleeping right now, and I just pulled myself from bed to turn off the lights I could see they'd left blazing everywhere, muttering to myself about how no one cares about a thing called global warming, and I caught one of them sneaking down the stairs for a bedtime snack. Nope. This is not an open-all-night diner. Although, if it were, I'd order myself a giant margarita.

Guess I'll have to be okay with another handful of chocolate chips.

Lifestyle Change didn't have six kids.

What It's Like Having More Than One Kid

Once upon a time, parenting was so easy. Husband and I would put something away—say, thumb tacks or permanent markers or, perhaps, a blue gel pen—and it remained put away. Tucked inside a cabinet somewhere, safe from little hands. I could, once upon a time, control every square foot of crawling space where my baby would happily scoot across carpet while examining every piece of lint or speck of dirt or forgotten crumb, or, because not many of those things existed in our meticulously cleaned space, his amazing hands.

It was easy, once upon a time, because he was the only one.

Now, when I get down on my knees to cheat through my pushups and stand back up when I've done as many as I can do —which tops out at about twenty—my kneecaps are sporting all kinds of unidentifiable grossness. (Why do I still do it? I don't know.)

Yesterday I picked up what looked like ancient popcorn kernels, tiny pieces of confetti-like paper, and mostly hair.

It doesn't matter if I just vacuumed ten seconds ago, I will never be disappointed by the epic nature of the grossness sticking to the sweat on my kneecaps (yes, my kneecaps sweat. Pushups are hard.). Someone in my house sheds like a Siberian

Husky cursed to spend the summer in Texas, and it's probably me.

It's not just old food particles and minuscule paper pieces and hair that burrow down into the fibers of carpet and resurface when I decide to make an effort to work out (beyond chasing kids, that is); it's also the astonishing number of things my sons leave on the floor. When I only had one son, I was able to manage this just fine. When he took off his jacket, I helped him hang it up where it went. When he decided he didn't want to wear socks with his tennis shoes, no problem; we could make sure those smelly socks made it to one of the three hampers situated strategically throughout my house. When he wanted to draw a picture of a flying elephant, he put the supplies away.

The problem is that now there are six little boys tearing off their socks and digging things out and forgetting they ever knew how to put things away. And shedding. (How can I be responsible for this massive volume of hair all by myself? Someone must be helping behind the scenes.)

The other problem is, my youngest son is now old enough to crawl but not old enough to distinguish between what's okay to pick up and what's not at all meant for his hands. When he finds dirty, smelly socks on the floor, they go in his mouth. When he finds important school papers spread on the floor, they go in his mouth. When he finds balls of hair they go—you guessed it!—in his mouth. Which means I have to vacuum every day. Which is probably what I should have been doing in the first place, but who wants to clean a house where seven males live? Not me.

Vacuuming every day does not take care of this problem in its entirety. Vacuums don't suck up things like the insides of a stuffed animal the three-year-olds thought it would be funny to de-fluff. Vacuums don't get rid of dirty underwear no one claims (I could tell to whom it belonged if I wanted to pick it up, but I'm not sure I do). It doesn't clear away left-out colored pencils.

What typically happens when you have more than one kid is that the three-year-old will decide he wants to color, so he'll get out the crayons and the colored pencils and his coloring book, because of course you keep all of that where he can reach it easily; art expression is important in your house—and it's a better alternative to butter-knife sword fighting with his imaginary friend, which has often been his preference but is definitely not allowed in your house. And then when this ingenious three-year-old is finished coloring thirty seconds later because he has the attention span of a squirrel, he goes straight for the trains even though the rule in your house is "one thing out at a time." So then you have The Cleanup Fight, which usually just means a three-year-old angrily swiping everything that was previously on the table onto the floor, screaming that he is "not going to clean them up and you're a mean booty-face" and then collapsing into a pile of noodles right beside the tantrum mess, hopefully scraping his back on one of those colored pencils so you can bring home the point that "that's what happens when you [blank]." And then he'll say he didn't get these pencils out in the first place—you did—and, besides, he didn't color with them, nu-uh, he didn't, and while you're reminding him that you were right beside him while he did exactly what he's saying he didn't, because you'll argue to the death with a three-year-old, your youngest son will pick up one of those pencils, slobber on it, and then try to get it in his mouth—because that's where everything's supposed to go.

For his efforts, he'll end up with a bright blue mural all over his face.

He was incredibly happy about his first taste of art.

His mother was not.

I cleaned him off and turned my attention back to the three-year-old, who was still boneless on the floor, pretending like he was too tired to clean up but not tired enough to lie down for his nap early. The nine-month-old promptly zeroed in on an old diaper Husband had left on the floor.

The moral of the story is: It's not just kids who complicate things; it's also Husbands.

I never knew the definition of madness until I welcomed more than one child into my home. But you know what else I never really knew?

Unbridled joy.

And if madness is the price I have to pay to experience even a moment of unbridled joy, then I will gladly do it all over again.

With balls of hair on my sweaty kneecaps.

So Much for a Yell-Free Year

This year, when I considered New Year's goals in relation to my family, I jotted down one I've never been able to quite accomplish: No yelling.

This goal has made it to the list just about every year since I've had a three-year-old. I've made progress, but there is always a situation that demands a little yell.

This year that situation presented itself at about 10 a.m. New Year's Day.

Husband and I make it no secret that we own a megaphone and use it frequently, because the noise six boys can make on a daily basis is like a thousand frightened elephants crashing through Stonehenge. The house trembles with the sound of it (and perhaps even in anticipation of it).

So in order for our hourly instructions to be heard over all this trumpeting and stomping and crashing and shrieking, we make sure our house is well stocked with Energizer D batteries and the megaphone is within reach of parent hands (definitely not kid hands. They don't need any help in the Department of Louder Voices).

So, on the rare occasion that the megaphone is nowhere to be found, or the batteries have run out and there are no more, yelling is necessary. Yelling to be heard above the voices of boys when they're shoving each other in some kind of game they call Enjoyable. Yelling to be heard over their whispers, even, when they're telling secrets (my sons are the loudest whisperers I've ever heard in my life). Yelling to get their attention, yelling to save them from dying, yelling to announce that dinner's ready, if their noses haven't already brought them inside.

I'm not talking about this kind of yelling. This kind of yelling is necessary, at least in my home.

No, I'm talking about the kind of yelling that grabs the fire of anger and flings it at walls and doors and, mostly, kid-faces.

Husband and I try really, really hard not to do this at all—but it seemed like we'd increased the yelling of late. We're not angry people, but boys, six of them, can quite often be maddening people. And, honestly, we're a little worn out. And we'd sometimes had enough of "whatever" before the kids had had enough. And there are a thousand excuses.

But when we looked around at our children during their two weeks (and an extra day!!!!) off from school, we realized (yet again) that yelling is not the answer. It's true that sometimes we didn't get enough sleep, because we had too much on our mind or the baby woke with a snot tree growing from his nose or the nine-year-old burst through our bedroom at 3 a.m. to say his tummy hurt five seconds before yesterday's roasted chicken breasts splattered my face (they are definitely more moist the second time around). It's true that money's tight right now and Husband and I are building careers from the ground up and we're balancing household responsibilities and we're raising six boys (!) who don't often understand what it means to "just be quiet, please. For one second so I can think."

I didn't want to be that parent, though. I had a parent who yelled at me when I was a kid, and even though he said things that were different in both subject and intention, the trauma of it still haunts me.

Before the New Year rolled around, Husband and I sat our sons down at the table and asked them what in the world their daddy and I could possibly do besides yelling (even the necessary kind). We often do this with our sons; we call it a Family Council, and you'd be surprised how many solutions our kids have come up with that actually work. We had high hopes for this meeting, too.

We asked more questions: How could we get their attention? What would make them stop and listen? How could we better express our momentary anger? What could boys do that might help parents do that might help boys do (because this parent-child relationship is a symbiotic cycle—the good kind, the kind that makes you both better)?

We made our plan. We put it in place.

And failed on Day One.

We can tear ourselves up about something like this. Our failure can make us believe we're not really good parents, because we slipped up that one time today, or those two times or those five thousand times. Failure can point fingers, make us feel, too, like maybe our kid will be forever messed up because we can't seem to make it through a nighttime routine, with its endless getting out of bed thousands of times by every single one of them, without yelling at them to "JUST STAY PUT FOR GOD'S SAKE."

But the truth is, we'll never be perfect parents, because we'll never be perfect people. We will only ever be *good enough* parents. *Good enough* people.

There are people who will tell us or make us feel like we should be perfect. They're wrong. Perfect is an illusion—one that steals the joy from life. From parenting. From entire families, if we let it.

I'm not saying it's a mistake not to make it our goal to stop yelling. It's great to have a plan and put that plan in place. It's great to take steps along the journey to where we want to be—to be ever improving as a parent and a person and a human being.

But we will never, ever, not even on our best days, do anything perfectly. Be perfect. We're humans who are raising humans, and that alone eliminates the possibility.

So we can stop making ourselves feel so bad for being imperfect people, for messing up, for not executing perfectly that admirable yet sometimes impossible goal. We can stop beating ourselves up for our failures.

You know what we get to do when we yell because our kids are losing their minds with the LEGOs, tossing them all up into the air like monkeys throwing poo and we don't really want to take down our ponytail tonight and feel the fourteen tiny little dragon-claw pieces spill out onto a floor and disappear to places where they'll be found in the dead of night during a half-asleep trip to the bathroom? We get to show our kids what it looks like to make amends. Repair what may have been broken. Fix a relationship and move into deeper and more meaningful conversation.

We get to show our kids what it looks and sounds like to offer an apology for a mistake we made (because yelling is a mistake in my personal parenting playbook).

We get to show them that we aren't perfect, so they don't have to be perfect, either.

I feel better already.

Toys and Kids: a Short Examination

As we near the holidays, when parents will probably spend more on their kids than they do at any other time of year, toy makers put their best foot forward: they release all the new and never-seen-before toys. My sons are not exposed to commercials, because we don't watch traditional television, only Netflix or Prime video on occasion (it's a different world, isn't it?), so, thankfully, my kids only hear about these new and never-seen-before toys when they're visiting their grandparents for Thanksgiving and we turn on the Macy's Thanksgiving Parade, which I haven't seen since I was a kid.

My sons wanted every toy advertised on the commercials.

It was quite humorous listening to them. "I want that for Christmas," they'd say, until the next commercial flashed on the screen and they said, "No, I want *that* for Christmas."

I can't imagine having this endless one-sided conversation all the time.

In my limited study I noticed that all the new and never-seen-before toys had a few things in common.

First: They are annoying.

My definition of annoying might be different from another parent's definition. What I mean by annoying is that these new and never-seen-before toys needed batteries in order to make their loud sounds and flash their brilliant lights. My experience with toys like these in my home is that eventually the batteries die, and Husband and I don't replace them, because, again, noises and lights are annoying. And because the noises and lights were the only reasons our sons played with them at all, they will inevitably abandon these toys, which allows me to promptly place them in a box to drop off at Goodwill on my way to the grocery store.

Unlike their parents, my sons never get tired of hearing the same thing over and over again, judging by the number of times I have to say, "Please shut the door" when they go outside or come back in.

There is also the kind of annoying that does not need batteries. Have you ever had a kid-sized drum set in your house? I have. It does not have a kid-sized sound. I felt like my sons were beating my head with their drumsticks every time they tried to play a song. That toy didn't last long.

And, of course, there is also the annoying that comes with a billion pieces. Puzzles, LEGO sets, or any kind of board game or matching game that look deceptively entertaining and thrilling until you take your eyes off your kid and he decides he's going to make a new carpet for your living room. Which leads me to…

Second: They make a mess.

It doesn't matter if these new and never-seen-before toys come in one piece. My sons will take care of that by dismantling them; they'll turn one very large piece into a billion very small ones.

Not to mention the law of entropy: toys attract toys. That's not the *technical* law, but it's the only one that really matters in a house with kids. I could clean out the toys every day of my life, and my sons would still find a way to make a mess with their toys—also with their art supplies, their books, and their notebooks, all of which they will leave on the floor so I can gracefully trip over them and skin my nose on the side of the couch. It's a wonder I'm still alive.

I guess it would be more fair to say that the new and never-seen-before toys aren't the only toys that make a mess; all toys make a mess unless there are no kids around to play with them.

Third: They must be worth fighting over.

This is pretty much every toy that has ever been made. If it's not fight-worthy, it's not buy-worthy. We have a rule in our house that whoever gets the toy for a birthday or a holiday has the right to play with it exclusively for the first day, and then they can share if they want. And it doesn't matter if a toy is made for a two-year-old or a cat—the eleven-year-old will want to play with it.

The other day, my seven-year-old brought home a toy he'd bought for the cat at his school holiday market. My sons spent twenty minutes fighting over whose turn it was to try to make the cat turn upside down—that is, until the cheap toy broke with one swat of our cat's claws.

Then they used a sock.

One day they'll learn the economics of buying the best and not the most.

How an Introvert Raises Six Kids

I am a quiet introvert living in the middle of seven other people. Loud people. Active people. Needy people.

This isn't always easy for me. By dinnertime, most days, I can already feel the anxiety and dread creeping up the back of my neck, because not only am I already at capacity for word count today, I'm also at capacity for touch, smell, sight, and taste (because smell can often become taste in the presence of a malodorous boy).

And I know dinner. I've been having dinner with my sons since the first one was born nine yeas ago. That's a lot of practice and experience with catastrophe, accidents, and vocal volume.

I love my sons. So much sometimes that my heart feels like it might split my chest. There is, however, a point in my day where I've had enough of them—with everyone in the world; I don't discriminate—and I just need some time away.

So how is it that an introvert survives in a 1,900-square-foot house shared with seven people—all of them males?

I've come up with a few tactics over the years. Here are some of them.

Robot Voice

Whenever I have reached my limit on word count and

vocal volume, I'll start talking in Robot Voice. Usually this special voice says something along the lines of, "System malfunction. Too many people talking at one time." Typical examples of when this voice comes climbing out my mouth are when my sons are talking all over each other to tell me about what they built in Minecraft during their technology time—which I don't *really* need to know—and I feel like a target for pointed pickaxes; when my four-year-old is telling me, in astonishing detail, about the load he just deposited into the toilet, which I can smell from fifty feet away—there's no escaping it; and when they're simultaneously asking for dinner while complaining about it already.

Sometimes I have a little fun with my robot voice. I'll pretend I never had another voice, and I'll conduct an entire conversation as Rachel the Robot, which usually makes my sons so mad they stop talking to me in the first place. Mission accomplished.

Tea Kettle

Tea Kettle is a shrill (but somewhat soft) shrieking—much like the name, a tea kettle. Tea Kettle comes in handy when I'm feeling overwhelmed by something all my sons are doing, when I can't see to all their needs because they're being unreasonably needy all at the same time, or when they're asking too many consecutive questions that I haven't even had a chance to answer before they're firing back yet another. Rather than yelling or covering my ears or running from the room completely, I become Tea Kettle.

My sons know, by now, that Tea Kettle is synonymous with

Mama is Overwhelmed. They get really quiet. Their eyes widen. They wait.

And the blissful silence, even if it's momentary, gives me time to catch my breath, center myself, swallow the anxiety that's always waiting at the edges. Tea Kettle can now cool down, until the next overwhelmed moment (there will be others).

Hideout

The tactic known as Hideout doesn't always work well, because how do you hide out in a house with only 1,900 square feet? But desperate times call for desperate measures. Sometimes I will shove myself into the pantry, without the lights on, which works as long as one of my sons doesn't barge in looking for something to eat (in a house of boys, this means I have only a couple of minutes to hide in the pantry).

Sometimes Hideout is executed in my closet, until one of my sons comes knocking because he wants to "look at" my sewing machine, which is really code for "steal thread from" my sewing machine (he must think I was born yesterday). I am apparently more observant than most of my children think; I know they're unraveling my thread so they can use the spools to create some contraption that will help them take over the world. And I found the unraveled thread in the four-year-old twins' room. They were tying one ecru end to their waists and the other to the doorknob and trying to see if they could open the door without turning the knob. They couldn't, because the thread was too long; it had been a brand new spool my son stole. My twins had marks all over their bellies from the thread; I thought it was a good lesson learned. At least until, two days later, I caught them trying it with black thread.

Some kids never learn.

A Screaming Pillow

A Screaming Pillow comes in handy when Robot Voice is too mild, Tea Kettle is too ineffective, and Hideout cannot be found, at least not for an adequate amount of time (five minutes, at least). In such cases, I will scream into a pillow while my sons look on in horror or astonishment—it's impossible to tell which. They don't know what to say, which is precisely the right thing to say—nothing. They'll stare at me and slowly filter out of the room.

Now I'm alone. Oh, bliss.

The Screaming Pillow can also be used when there's something I'd like to say but know I shouldn't. No sense in wounding a child. Just say the words into the pillow; they'll never be able to decode the muffled lines. They can hardly decode my clear lines, judging by how few times they follow the directions I give.

Crazy Eyes

For you to understand the full marvel of Crazy Eyes, I must first describe them to you. Executing Crazy Eyes is really very simple. All a parent has to do is open their eyes really wide—and I mean really wide. You must, however, make sure you don't raise your eyebrows while opening your eyes really wide; this just makes you look surprised and can be mistaken for interest on the part of your children. Crazy Eyes are wide eyes with no eyebrows raised and no other expression on your face beyond blankness. Just plain and simple eyes. Your eyes are going to swallow your face. Your eyes are going to swallow *them*.

I don't use my Crazy Eyes all that often, and when I do, it's only around dinnertime, when we're supposed to be sharing our highs and lows but no one is really listening to each other, because they can't decide who's supposed to go first, even though we already named the kid who's supposed to go first. It's like they only hear the question but never the name that's attached to it.

Crazy Eyes also occasionally make their appearance when the nine-year-old is using four billion words to tell me about his latest adventure in Five Nights at Freddy's, and (1) I could have summed that up in two hundred words and (2) I have a really hard time caring about Five Nights at Freddy's.

Do Not Disturb Sign

I use this sign on myself. I wear it around my neck. Not that it helps. My sons will still latch onto my legs and ride me around the living room. They will still seek me out for conversation. They will still paw all over me because they missed me so much during the day, oh, and also they want to show me this world they created during their tech time today, or they want to read me this really funny (not really funny) joke they read in a Garfield book or they want to make up their own joke that doesn't make the least bit of sense but now I have to laugh to be nice.

I still wear it. Because one day they'll be able to read and understand. And then I probably won't need it. Oh, well.

Book Head

Sometimes I'll walk around with a book in front of my face. It's not that I'm reading, because how can you read in a house full of clowns? It's just that it's another message for them: steer clear of Mama.

This one rarely works. But I am not a quitter.

My Own Chair

My Own Chair is a beat-up chaise we have in our home library. Sometimes my sons will climb onto my lap, and I won't be able to see the story I'm reading because their head's blocking the page. Sometimes they'll notice that I'm reading slowly, because I have to keep looking around their heads, so they'll slide off my lap and sit beside me instead (only a couple of my sons are so observant). But this chair always remains my chair. If anyone happens to be sitting in it when I emerge from my room for story hour, the first thing I say is "Please get out of My Own Chair." They look at me to see if I'm serious. Then they move.

This seat is mine.

Supportive Partner

This is probably the most important piece of keeping an introvert sane in a house of people. Husband is one of the most supportive people in the world. He loves me. He not only believes wholeheartedly in my pursuits and encourages me to work outside the home, but he's a real dad. He takes initiative to be in his kids' lives in a very present way, and one of those ways is offering me no-payback breaks when he can see I'm about to break.

Apologies

I mess up. So much. That means I've gotten really good at apologizing to my kids.

It's not hard to mess up when you're walking around in a state of constant overstimulation and overwhelm. Thankfully, my kids are really great at forgiving, too.

It is never simple or easy to be an introverted mother of six boys, but these tactics help. And it's important to show my sons how I care for myself—because some of them are introverts, too, and the most important thing introverts must learn is that the world cannot have us all the time. Rest and renewal is essential.

So when I close my door and hang up my Do Not Disturb sign, they learn that they have permission to do it, too.

Which is well worth the effort. Especially since I get to be alone.

Oh, bliss.

What Parents Do When Their Kids Aren't Around

The other day I contracted a stomach virus through which I had successfully nursed my sons, and during my morning shift with the littles, I laid down flat on the floor and tried to live. My stomach was knotted up tight, and all I really wanted to do was take a nap. But all my sons wanted was lunch. So lunch it was.

Husband and I haven't had a day away from our children in much too long. Months without even a date night start weighing on a parent. Parenting is relentless. It's hard on a marriage, hard on an individual, hard on a life. There's no day off—even when you're sick, you have to address behavior issues, keep sons out of the refrigerator, and listen to them complain about the dinner you cooked in between your retching.

Every now and then, though, Husband and I are fortunate enough to take a weekend away from the kids, because our parents start noticing our wild-eyed looks and decide maybe it's time to intervene and save us (thanks, parents!). Every parent needs this temporary time away, because it's a time of blissful rest when you don't have to buckle kids if you decide to go somewhere on a whim and you can talk to each other without a hundred voices tripping over yours.

Here are some of the things Husband and I do outside of our kids' presence:

Sleep

Most of the time we're so exhausted that even though we would like nothing more than to sit up late and talk the way we used to do pre-kids, we settle into our bed for good conversation and are promptly snoring—or at least I am. And the sleep is nice, because there are no children who may potentially burst into our room in the middle of the night and make me think someone's come to murder us—which is always where my mind first goes. Wouldn't you like to be me?

Talk

Husband and I actually get to have a normal conversation when we're not immediately falling asleep. This conversation is so efficient, compared to all the others when a kid will interrupt a train of thought with a polite but annoying, "Excuse me, Mama" or "Excuse me, Daddy" as soon as we open our mouths to download what's been circulating in our brains for days—sometimes months. That's how long it takes to "find a good time" when you have kids. But no time is ever a good time if the kids are present. I have no idea how they know when their parents are about to talk about something important, but they sure do.

Read

When the kids are gone, I can read one page one time, instead of one page five times. I can immerse myself fully in another entertaining world. I can crack open a book without fear of a boy cracking open my head when he decides my lap looks like a nice landing pad for this leap off the couch.

Take a shower

There are so many things that can happen when a parent steps into a shower—no matter how short it is. Once, when I got tired of my greasy hair, I decided to take a two-minute shower (even set a timer). I returned downstairs to find my kids seated around Monopoly, Risk, and Go Fish, all the pieces artfully arranged in a fashionable board game throw rug. After I sliced my toe on a Lord of the Rings Risk goblin figure and discovered that there were also, delightfully, ten pounds of bananas gone and the six-year-old turned to me with a blue face and told me he had no idea who had eaten the bananas or the blueberries, I decided that even a two-minute shower wasn't worth it. Next time I'd spray down my hair in the kitchen sink.

Eat out

When Husband and I don't have the kids at home, we will eat out nearly every night they're with grandparents. We do this for two practical reasons:

a. Once you're used to cooking for a household of eight people, you forget how to cook for two.

b. It's the only time we can do it without slapping down our entire grocery budget for the month, because feeding eight people a restaurant meal is not cheap. Husband and I are cheap, though, so we save the restaurant meals for when kids are gone.

Sit down for more than two seconds

When I try to sit down while all the kids are home, someone will tell me I forgot to pour them milk this morning, someone needs me to wipe uranus (that is not a typo, and we're not talking about the planet), and someone else wants the hidden LEGOs out. Not to mention, as soon as I sit down I fall asleep. You don't want to see what kids do when a parent accidentally falls asleep on duty.

Take your time

With kids, it seems that everywhere we go is hurry, hurry, hurry. This is because kids do everything slowly—especially putting on their shoes (if they can find them in the first place). But when Husband and I are on our own, we can not only leave the house in record time, but we can also linger over the museum display without worrying that one of the four-year-olds will wander off into the indigenous people display and come back wearing only a loincloth.

Talk about the kids

Everywhere we go on a kidless weekend, we talk about our sons and how much we miss them, even though as soon as we pick them up from grandparents we'll be ready for the next weekend away. But this is part of the treasure of weekends without children—we remember why we love each other so much and we remember how very much we love our sons.

Mostly we remember that we would not want our life any other way.

The Lamentable Principles of My Kids' Tooth Fairy

One school morning, my third son woke up uncharacteristically cantankerous. This kid is generally like a grumpy bear in the mornings, but this particular morning he was more like a bear who'd been woken from hibernation three minutes before he was supposed to be woken. (I imagine that bear would be upset; I feel upset every time I wake up three minutes before my alarm goes off.)

He stalked around the house grumbling under his breath. I tried to listen, but I couldn't quite make out anything of note. I assumed he'd feel better after breakfast, but he sat at the breakfast table and moped.

"Everything okay, baby?" I said.

He shook his head.

"Want to talk about it?"

He shook his head.

I try not to pry. I like to let them talk when they're ready, but something was clearly bothering him, so I said, "You didn't sleep all that well?" intending to utilize the process of elimination, which generally works for a seven-year-old.

"I slept just fine," he said in decidedly snappy voice.

I cocked my head, squinted my eyes, stirred the oatmeal.

Waited.

He said, "The tooth fairy didn't leave me any money." He held up something tiny. It was a tooth.

Oh, no.

I likely should have known, immediately, what was wrong; this is a standard happenstance in our home. Someone loses a tooth—someone is always losing a tooth, it seems—puts it under their pillow with high hopes for prosperity, and they wake up the next morning to nothing but the tooth.

The tooth fairy has been a *bit* flaky in our home.

Who would have ever thought the tooth fairy could be so complicated? I sure never did.

In our house, teeth fall out every other day (that's a slight exaggeration—but only slight), but the tooth fairy very rarely visits.

There are a variety of reasons for this: She doesn't carry cash, she's much more forgetful than she used to be (she's very old by now), and the tooth can't always be found.

Husband and I always warn whichever boy has lost the tooth to leave it in a certain place where it will be easy to find when they go to bed and need to transfer it to the spot under their pillow. But the problem is that there is always an abundance of curious brothers manhandling that tooth with a bloody bit of root attached to it; they think it's the most amazing thing. They don't always remember to put it back where it was.

I'm convinced that someone in my house (certainly not the tooth fairy) has a tooth repository somewhere, and it likely looks like something out of a horror film. I haven't found it yet, and I'm glad. Creepy kids.

The cost of teeth these days is incredible. It seems that inflation has ballooned the prize that kids expect to be waiting beneath their pillow when they wake after a visit from the tooth fairy. My sons come home talking about how the tooth fairy left twenty dollars under their friend's pillow, and they're all excited about this because they think it will happen to them, too. My poor kids don't realize that there are different tooth fairies working the world and the tooth fairy assigned to our house does *not* leave twenty-dollar bills. She usually leaves an IOU—or nothing. So disappointing.

I'm pretty sure that some of my kids have prematurely stopped believing in the tooth fairy because of our shortcomings, but, well, what can you do. Parenting is hard even without all the required extras.

In the last four years, the tooth fairy assigned to our home has demonstrated some of her principles. You've already heard one of them: She doesn't adjust much for inflation. Kids get five dollars for losing their first tooth (maybe) and a dollar every tooth after that. I'd say this is enough adjustment for inflation; I got a quarter for every tooth when I was a kid (and I tell my kids this every chance I get—they're lucky). So even though a kid can't buy much for a dollar, that's as much as our tooth fairy will splurge. If my sons would actually save their dollars in a piggy bank or something, they'd have thirty-two dollars by the time it was all over.

The future, unfortunately, doesn't mean that much to them

yet.

The tooth fairy is also usually late. This is because she has a billion things going on in her house. She has kids she needs to send off to school, a house she needs to clean, clothes she needs to wash, work she needs to do, kids she needs to bathe and put down to bed, and, by the end of the evening, her brain and her body have been emptied out; not only does she not remember that someone lost a tooth, but she also has no energy left to lift herself from the bed, tiptoe down the hall, and slip a dollar underneath a pillow. Add to this exhaustion-complication the fact that the tooth fairy usually goes to bed before her older children do, so when would she sneak? True, she gets up at 4:15 every morning, but by that time she's definitely forgotten that someone lost a tooth.

It really is a tragic circumstance.

When my sons wake on a morning after losing a tooth, they first check their pillow, to their great disappointment. They next come storming into our room or down the stairs, wherever Husband or I happen to be. They then posit that one of their brothers must have stolen the money the tooth fairy left under their pillow, because there was nothing this morning when they checked, after which Husband and I will exchange a look and one or the other of us will say, "She just added it to your allowance."

"How much?" the boy will say.

We'll shrug. "A dollar," we'll say.

If they complain, we remind them that the tooth fairy *did* say their daddy or I could take the dollar and use it for ourselves if the recipient was not grateful, after which they will zip their mouth closed and be, perhaps, marginally grateful for a dollar they didn't have yesterday.

Husband and I don't put too much pressure on ourselves to keep up this ruse; it is, after all, a ruse. One of these days our sons will know why the tooth fairy doesn't always make it here on time. For now, we congratulate the son who's lost a tooth, examine the one coming in, and bask in that adorable gap-toothed grin.

And, in the backs of our minds, we continue hoping that we never, ever stumble across that nightmare stash of lost teeth.

Non-Traumatic Things that Might Make Parents Cry

If there's anything my kids would say about me as their mother (besides the fact that at least five times during the day I am the Worst Mother Ever—put-away-the-technology time, dinner time, chore time, bath time, and bedtime) is that I am a cryer. And I wouldn't be able to argue; I cry about everything, in every circumstance. I cry when I laugh, I cry when I feel angry or upset, I cry when I can't handle all the joy that's exploding from my life.

Even so, I suspect there are certain things that make parents cry that have nothing to do with the wonderful moments like a kid walking across a stage, a son pelting his mother with a flower, the first "I love you," every amazing achievement, a sweet movie watched with kids, a brilliant display of intelligence, a creative contribution to the world.

Here are some of the non-traumatic and definitely non-wonderful things that make parents cry:

The state of their house.

You could've recently spent the last six hours of your life cleaning and tidying your house, because your kids were away with their grandparents, and then they return home and it turns out it's possible to destroy a house in only thirty seconds.

This is life with kids. This is something worthy of breaking down into sobbing tears. You'll never get those six hours back. But you will certainly learn your lesson for the next time.

I'd like to pretend that this is only a hypothetical example, but I always try to be truthful in my essays. So I must confess that I cried sobbing tears this morning. There's a good reason for this—I stayed up way too late last night reorganizing a room while the kids were sleeping and I woke up this morning to a room that had been hit by a tornado.

My eyes are blurring just thinking about it.

The massive pile of laundry.

Every Monday, I stare at a massive pile of dirty laundry and feel the urge to cry. I want to cry because it's never ending, because I know that once this massive pile is done, there will be another pile waiting for me next week. Laundry is the one thing you can count on when you're a parent (well, that and never having any food when you want it because your sons are Hoovers).

The art cabinet.

I have labeled this cabinet. My sons know where everything goes, because it's written on masking tape with arrows conveniently pointing to the designated homes of glue or crayons or scissors.

To see this cabinet, you'd think I have no sons who can actually read. I assure you, I do. And if I have to spend another hour organizing this cabinet, I will drag it out to the curb and see who wants it for free.

(Not really. This cabinet belonged to my grandmother; it's

the only thing of hers I have left, besides pictures. So everything that's in it can go, and we'll just enjoy an empty cabinet, which seems like a luxury in a house of eight.)

Cleaning your house to have a birthday party.

I don't know why we do it. It takes three hours to clean this house—and that's not even a thorough cleaning, just a spot treatment, which is to say, the toilets. Maybe walls near the toilets. And the floors around the toilets.

This "cleaning" is mostly tidying, putting things where they go, giving the floors a vacuum that doesn't get rid of all the stains, piling things on the stairs if you're Husband. But even that effort is wasted; within minutes my nieces and nephews have joined my sons in decorating our house in the latest style: Toys with a Bit of Floor On the Side.

The floors, once everyone leaves, look like they haven't been vacuumed in years, so covered in cake crumbs and chip fragments are they. The counters are dappled with salsa and plastic cups everyone left out. The toilets are, well, you probably don't want to know.

Still I bother. Because people are coming over, and I like to pretend I have standards. (I used to. They've lowered immensely.)

Tech time.

If there's one thing that my sons and I fight about more than anything else, it's tech time. They don't want to stop when it's time to stop. They don't want to do what earns them tech time in the first place. They don't want to accept that tech time is a privilege, not a right.

When Husband and I take them out for a Family Fun Day and spend six hours carting them around the local zoo and a wooded park, they will whine on the way home about how they didn't get to have any tech time. When we're in the store, they will ask how long this is going to take, because they'd like to get home in time for tech time. They will skip dinner if it means they can have tech time.

All things considered, I cry more than they do about tech time.

Sometimes I think it would be easier not to monitor it, but I'm not yet willing to give up that fight.

The four billion cups they use in a day.

Another job that's never finished in a house of eight is washing dishes. While I hole away inside my room every afternoon to write essays and stories and poems, there must be a parade of people marching through my house (the constant jolting slam of the front and back doors supports this theory), because by the time I'm finished and down in my kitchen, the counter is lined with cups. I didn't even know we had this many cups. It'll take years to wash them.

I spend half my life washing dishes.

Searching for shoes.

I am all about treasure hunts. Give me a map with X marks the spot, and I will search until there is no searching left to be done.

Not so with searching for shoes. I hate searching for shoes. There is no treasure at the end of this search. There is only "Why are they here?"

In our home, we have baskets where our children are supposed to put their shoes as soon as they take them off, but do they ever get there? Sometimes, actually. Not most of the time, though. Which means most of the time, Husband and I are doing a mad dash around the house, trying to find the missing shoe. Or several.

Our searches sometimes only uncover left shoes, which means the kid with the missing right shoe will have to wear two left shoes and complain about it the entire time we're at the store.

The other day we were going to the zoo, and I told all my sons to get flip flops. I'm tired of tying shoes, and it's summer. Flip flops are standard uniform during a Texas summer. Socks don't dry in the summertime. Trust me. I've accidentally picked up a few while trying to shove clothes in the washer.

My five-year-old couldn't find both his brand new flip flops, so he wore mismatched ones. I don't even care. The odds of only one out of six wearing mismatched shoes is actually pretty good.

The empty refrigerator.

My sons eat a lot. So when my stomach and the noises it's making tell me it's time to come downstairs for a snack (which I only do once a day—and sometimes not even that), there is nothing left. They have, in the course of a day, eaten five pounds of apples and ten pounds of carrots. All I wanted was one apple or one carrot, but even that was too much to ask.

I guess it's better for the figure, but every now and then I'd really like a snack, kid.

Parenting is hard. Who says we have to do it without tears?

What I Imagine Would Happen if My Kids Were Home Alone

Husband and I have been eagerly awaiting the time when we will be able to leave our sons at home without parental supervision. The oldest just turned ten, but I'm thinking this rite of passage is still quite a way off. The other day, when he offered to watch his brothers for half an hour so Husband and I could go for a quick walk and I asked him what he would do with his brothers *if* we took him up on his offer, he said, "I'll just lock the twins in their room and then no one else is really a problem."

Clearly he doesn't understand what "babysitting" means.

He's a fairly responsible kid, but he's not all that observant. If his attention is stolen by anything—a bird in the backyard that he wants to identify, an idea that he has to act on right this very minute, a really good book—then the entire rest of the world is left to its own devices. He becomes efficiently and completely immersed in his own world.

The thought of having some time away while this son watches his brothers is very tempting. We don't get many date nights. And this kid is the one who once told my mother that he wished he could figure out how to clone Husband and me so that one set of us could watch him and his brothers while the other set got to go out on a date. He knows we're starved for dates and time alone, and he's sweet enough to care.

Still, I'm too smart to sign off on Temporary Head of Household just yet.

The problem isn't really him, either. The problem is that all six of my children are BOYS. Husband had a brother. I've heard insane stories about what brothers do together, and this does not help my son's case at all. My sister's husband had a brother, and his stories are even worse than Husband's. What their stories tell me (and what I know to be true already) is that the things boys do are impulsive and careless and, I hate to say —I really do—stupid. Every now and then Husband, my brother, or my brothers-in-law will provide me with a glimpse of the little boys who still live inside them.

Take the Fourth of July in 2011, for example. These fine grown men of my family—all of them fathers, mind you—decided that year that they would drop some cash on fireworks —but instead of setting the fireworks off at night, they would do it during the day, using a PVC pipe as a homemade bazooka. This ended almost as badly as you might imagine—a fire started in the field behind our home. Thankfully, my stepdad, at the time, was a volunteer firefighter, and he managed to get it under control before anybody else knew of their prank. I don't think I've ever seen him move that fast before, and I've known him since I was twelve.

This is exactly what leads me to believe that it's quite possible I will never be able to leave my sons home alone.

Recently I asked this question on social media: What age is

old enough for children to stay home alone? I got a variety of answers. None of my friends had a definitive one, because it's really up to the parents and the kids. I know this. I remember staying home alone when I was eight, my brother was nine, and my little sister was five—but I was an old woman trapped in a child's body. Also, there was only one boy.

Here's what I imagine would happen if my sons stayed home alone for any amount of time:

1. Someone would surely get hurt.

This is because someone would most likely decide to do something ridiculous, like climb to the top of the deck covering, which isn't as high as the roof, and jump off with a trash bag they still think can make them fly; that someone might break his leg. Or someone would decide it might be fun to sword fight with butcher knives, since Mama and Daddy have always forbidden it and they're the worst parents ever and only want kids to not have any fun; this someone might have his nose lobbed off. Or someone else would try to walk on the roof with their roller blades strapped to their feet because the slope of it makes the perfect ramp. That someone might break every bone in his body.

Boys think they're invincible. Especially when they're alone with no parent to talk any sense into them.

2. All the food would vanish.

When my sons are home, the most frequent phrase I repeat, besides, "You've already asked that question and I've already answered it," is, "Get out of the refrigerator." I suspect that as soon as Husband and I were to walk out of sight or drive away (one day), our boys would immediately open up the fridge and binge on the rest of whatever's there.

We'd likely either come home to a completely empty refrigerator or a bunch of boys in prone positions complaining their stomachs hurt because they ate ten pounds of bananas on a dare or they found my hidden chocolate reserves or they drank a whole gallon of milk to see who could drink it the fastest without puking out their insides—which is what the boys in my church youth group used to do for fun on the weekends. They always did it at night, when their milk vomit practically glowed in the dark. Night or day, it was still stupid.

You'll notice a recurring theme here.

3. They'd fight and one would threaten to run away—and actually accomplish it.

Since this happens often when Husband and I are home, I imagine that the same would happen if we were away for any length of time. The missing variable is Parent, but if there's a Substitute Parent, I foresee it still being a problem.

And my sons don't just threaten to run away: they do.

We live in a relatively safe neighborhood, and they have friends living all around it, so when they say they'll run away, they'll usually just go hang out at a friend's house up at the top of the cul-de-sac. They're easy enough to find; I let them have their momentary victory while observing their imagined escape.

But when a brother is in charge, he would probably not be quite so inclined to watch and "find" his missing brother, since the impetus to running away was the fight they just had.

Brother In Charge despises Brother Who Ran.

The problem is not so neatly resolved.

4. Something terrible would befall the house.

Everywhere my sons go in my house, they leave their marks behind. There are fingerprints on windows and holes in the walls and ski marks on the carpet (don't ask). One of them the other day "accidentally" slammed the back door too hard, and a picture frame fell off the wall and shattered at his feet. He was shocked to know that he had such power.

Boys, as any parent knows, don't think about the fact that if they climb onto a bookshelf full of books, it might actually fall over (if it's not bolted to the wall—and sometimes even then). If they try to stack two chairs on top of each other, even when the makeshift "stool" is propped against a wall, they will still fall and, for their efforts, punch a new hole in the wall. If they try to do a pull-up on the open cabinet, that cabinet will rip from its hinges.

They don't think about what they're doing until there's a gaping hollow in the door where they thought it would be funny to kick it closed. They don't think about what they're doing until there's a shower curtain bent in two, because they wanted to see if it could actually support their weight. They don't think about what they're doing until the mirror is shattered in front of them because they thought it would be funny to throw a metal car at it.

Without parents at home, all my house's protection vanishes.

If my sons were left alone, the chance that they would do

something stupid and irresponsible increases, by default, by about one thousand percent.

Everybody knows that boys need the loving hand of a wise parent to keep them from doing something reckless. They only have the capacity to consider how cool the idea would be. You want to see what it would be like to jump from the roof to the trampoline? I'm game. You want to ride a skateboard down the stairs? Yep. Me too. You want to set off firecrackers from a PVC pipe? Let's do it.

What could possibly go wrong?

Every now and then, my ten-year-old will try again. He'll tell us to go ahead and go out on a date. He'll take care of his brothers—for a price (ten dollars. He has a cheap going rate). We thank him for his kindness and consideration and politely decline for now.

And, possibly, forever (but I really hope not).

No Sane Parent Ever Did it All

There are many times when I'm out and about with all my sons, and people get a good look at the wild spectacle we make wherever we go. Someone is probably getting left behind because he wanted to bring a billion things with him and now his backpack is too heavy to carry, and he's nearly toppling over backwards. Someone else probably has on mismatched shoes. At least one of them is likely shouting that he needs to go potty.

They say the only thing you can depend on in life is that it changes—but these things, for me, very rarely change. When I say I like stability and routine, I am not referring to Mr. Lag-Behind, Mr. Fashion Faux Pas, or Mr. Pottyman above.

Some people, of course, can be somewhat rude when they see a troupe like mine tripping down the street. Others are sweet. And still others seem to be completely amazed that there exists a woman with all these boys and *she is still standing*.

I'm amazed most days, too.

What these amazed observers will typically say, in one way or another, is: "I don't know how you do it all."

I have to physically restrain myself from laughing.

The truth is, I don't know how you do it all, either—

because I don't.

There are actually a whole lot of things I don't do, and because this phrase is probably the most frequent one I hear from other mothers of fewer children, I need to set it straight that I am no supermom.

Here are the things I don't actually do.

1. Clean

If you are lucky (or unlucky, depending on your outlook) enough to walk inside my house, don't look too closely at the baseboards or the bookshelves or the fan blades, if the fan isn't on, throwing its two inches of dusty matter all over the living room. I try to keep the fan on so people aren't enamored by how it's still connected to the ceiling with all that dust weighing it down.

I don't invite many people over—not because I wouldn't love having people over, in moderation, but because I'm a little embarrassed about how infrequently I clean. I work a full-time job and I have six children and our weekends are usually spent playing together. Or sometimes working, because I work from home, and that means there are lots of interruptions, which means work often doesn't get done in its entirety.

A couple of years ago, Husband and I thought, for about a second, that we might be able to slide in one Saturday a month where we could mobilize our male army to do a deep cleaning of the house, but, upon experimentation and failed execution, we realized the laughable futility of this plan. Not only is it impossible to supervise kids while they're cleaning ("Don't spray that in your brother's mouth!") it is also impossible to supervise kids while I am cleaning. Plus, I'm exhausted by the time the weekend rolls around. It's just easier to get out there and play a game of dodge ball against the four-year-olds who sassed me this morning.

In fact, you could say that the state of our house is a testament to our exhaustion. There are milk stains on the couches, where kids have wiped their gaping mouths for some reason or another; there are streaks on the underside of the kitchen table, where sons have smeared their hands (at least they didn't use their shirts!); and there are smudges on the bathroom walls where the boys have wiped their…well, I don't really know what. I probably don't want to.

2. Volunteer

Every now and then I feel the same guilt that probably every mother feels when they deliver their kids to school—right before the blissful relief sets in. The flash of guilt says: *You should be playing with them at school every chance you get.*

Every chance? I don't know. That seems like a lot of playing.

But this guilt is persistent. It likes to say that I should be going to all my kids' parties and scheduling lunch with them and volunteering to participate in every extra activity that the school initiates, which seems to be more and more every year.

The problem is that if I did this—if I volunteered for everything—I would never get any work done. And while my kids would love to see me at their school Christmas party, I believe they would likely be more inclined to have food to eat every day. My work helps put food on the table, and, at the end of the day, that's all that matters to growing boys.

Not only that, but I am a saner person when I have a career to pursue.

And, full disclosure (because I think it's important to tell the truth): taking someone else's kids to the children's museum for a class field trip doesn't sound exactly enjoyable. Thanks but no thanks.

3. Laundry

Oh, laundry. (Imagine that said in a moaning croak.)

Laundry is my nemesis. To be clear, I do eight loads of laundry every week (wouldn't want my sons running around in dirty underpants, or, worse, no underpants at all). I have plans to slowly teach each son to take care of his own laundry. Teach him the blessing of clean clothes. Initiate him into the I Hate Laundry Club. It's a fun club to join—it doesn't require monetary dues and your membership lasts a lifetime, even if you want to escape it.

The problem, in my house, isn't *doing* laundry, it's putting laundry away. Our laundry stays in piles—not even neat ones, because kids are pulling shirts and underwear and pants out of piles—on the banister that lines the hallway between my bedroom and our home library—the only hallway I can take to get downstairs. Which means I get to look at this lovely laundry pile every time I emerge from my bedroom to tell my sons to get back in bed, which, by my calculations, is about thirteen times every evening. That may be a conservative estimate.

My sons are responsible for putting away their own

clothes. Do they? That's questionable. It depends on what you mean by "put clothes away." If you mean "stuff them in your closet" or "shove them into any available drawer," then, yes, my sons are quite accomplished at putting their clothes away.

Hey, at least I don't have to look at it lining my banister.

4. Hover

I apologize if this is a bit offensive, but I do not supervise my children every minute of every day. There are too many to supervise every minute of every day. If I were to hold this expectation of myself, I would also require three clones. And, we may as well say it, sometimes I just need a break from Boy.

I am not the kind of mother who has the time or energy to follow all my sons around every minute of every day to make sure they're not doing something they shouldn't. I trust them, mostly. And when they break that trust, we have a talk, they have a consequence, and I fortify my vigilance for that one child. Until then, they're big boys. They're quite adept at self-management (which they only develop with practice).

5. Cook dinner

In my family, we don't eat out. We also don't eat processed foods. So how is it that I get away with not cooking dinner? Well, mostly this is because Husband does the dinner cooking; it's how we've arranged our schedules. But when it's my turn to prepare dinner, which comes around three days a week, I still rarely cook.

No, I'm not feeding my kids raw eggs. But I am feeding them raw carrots and raw kiwi and raw celery, because sometimes you just have to go the easy route and give them what nature made without softening it up. Food doesn't have to be cooked all the time. There's even a diet lifestyle called the Raw Food Diet, which I would adopt if I wasn't also fond of eggs every now and then. Raw eggs could cause problems.

My sons don't mind this kind of dinner so much, as long as they're eating *something*. Fortunately, they love carrots and kiwi and celery; they'll probably even ask for seconds.

6. Remember

There are so many things I don't remember. Last night I forgot to start the dishwasher, because Husband said something interesting and I was feeling celebratory that I'd finally waded through the thirty-five cups my kids dirtied in the course of one day. So the dishes were dirty when I opened the dishwasher this morning. I gave my kids yogurt in the bean bowls anyway. They didn't even notice, they were inhaling so fast.

Starting the dishwasher is only one line on the ever-growing list of things I don't remember. I don't always remember to send an apple to school when my six-year-old is studying apples in science. I don't always remember to brush my hair before I head up to the school and drop off my sons at their teachers' doors (and I don't actually notice until I come back home, because life is a whirlwind, not a dream). I don't always remember to pluck that rather thick black chin hair I noticed yesterday before heading confidently out into the public.

I don't always remember what day it is or why I came into this room or what I was trying to say before someone (probably a child) interrupted me. Remembering has become a lost art.

7. Friends

This is a *bit* of an exaggeration, though not much. I don't have many friends. Once a month, I get together with a group of ladies for a book club meeting, because this is all we can manage with our busy schedules. I hardly have any other contact with the outside world. The best I can do is wave to a few friends on social media once or twice a week and then retreat into my mother hole again. Parenting is a lonely pursuit.

The real truth, for all of us, is that we can't possibly do it all. We'll have to make concessions. One of my concessions is that I can't have a clean house twenty-four hours a day, seven days a week. I spend that time, instead, playing with my kids, because that's my priority.

I know what I can and cannot do. And I do only what I can do. We make parenting exponentially harder on ourselves when we try to do it all, when we reach for that impossible peak of perfection.

And I think we can all agree that parenting is already hard enough.

THE PARENTING LIFE'S A BIG MESS

What Silence Means in the Life of a Parent

Some days I long for silence. I feel the physical ache that I have come to recognize as the absence of silence. As an introspective person (and an introvert as well), silence gives me the space I need to reflect on my thoughts, to write, to read and simply be.

To hear my inner knowing.

But I am a parent.

When you are a parent, silence means something completely different than it meant to me when I was single or even newly attached. Silence then meant alone-time, a peaceful moment of relaxation, a blissful engagement with a book or a movie or a journal without any repercussions beyond time—an entire Saturday, perhaps—slipping away.

Silence turns darker when you become a parent. It resembles, now, something frightful, anxiety-filled, the kind of thing that makes me look over my shoulder to see what might be coming. I know that the longer the silence—the longer I take advantage of my idyllic moment alone—the worse the consequences of it will be.

Here are a few things silence means in my life as a mom:

1. Someone is missing.

This may be entirely unique to my family. I have six children. When one of them is missing from the group, it's like most of them are missing. It's the strangest thing. A couple of weekends ago, my in-laws took my oldest son on a birthday trip, and I have never heard that much silence in my house, with five kids in attendance. The ones remaining didn't know what to do with themselves while their brother was gone. It was somewhat charming to know that they, too, feel a hole when a family member is missing.

But when I know that all six of my sons are home and not with their grandparents, I know that silence means someone has probably walked out the front door, on silent steps and, for once, without slamming the door, without asking permission. They're probably up the hill at a friend's house and just forgot to tell me where they were going. But the silence swells inside me, growing larger than the back of my throat (because I'm also an anxious person) and I will call in the search party—which is a ready-made six-person team, minus the two who don't follow instructions and the one who is too young to search—and we'll all commence shouting and calling for the missing one. He'll emerge with a shell-shocked expression on his face. I don't blame him. The search party calls are the very opposite of silence. I can hardly even tell what his name is, so uncoordinated are our calls.

2. Someone's doing something they're not supposed to.

Husband and I had just put our twins and baby down for a nap the other day, leaving two of our older sons downstairs alone. We were in our bedroom finalizing a grocery pickup order, when I felt the silence creep up my shoulders and start pressing down on the back of my neck. It was a very physical, tangible sensation, the kind of tension that seems to tie knots in muscles. I thought, *I should go check on the boys.*

And, indeed, I should have, instead of powering through and finishing that grocery order. Our sons were making elaborate paper monsters with scrapbook paper and sharp scissors. One of them had glued a corner of his shirt to the table without noticing. Every time he tried to step away, the table ripped him back. The other had glued a red owl in his hair, just to see what it would look like. And, best of all, the dining room table and floor around it were covered in tiny little paper scraps. My favorite.

Another time, I went to dump out laundry on my bed. I was gone for maybe two minutes. When I came back down the stairs, I was greeted by the faces of three lions, courtesy of one of the four-year-olds and a permanent marker.

Silence is not golden in a house of children.

3. Someone is eating.

Periodically, on a Saturday, Husband and I will lie down for a fifteen-minute power nap. You think nothing much can go wrong in fifteen minutes, but you'd be wrong. During that time, about which we also alert our children so they don't interrupt our nap (this is probably the problem), the house settles into a miraculous silence. Though we know better by now, Husband and I always tell ourselves that our sons are embracing this silence so their parents will be able to nap better.

Nope.

We'll come downstairs to see that five pounds of apples have been consumed, along with two pounds of strawberries, four pounds of carrots, and yesterday's rice casserole. They were quiet because they were shoveling food in their faces.

Well, at least the apples and rice casserole will balance out the explosive diarrhea.

4. Someone is sleeping.

This is best-case scenario. It shouldn't even be on the list; I'll take any silence that means my sons are sleeping.

I have to confess that sometimes I'm pleasantly surprised by what the silence in my house means. Sometimes—actually, if I'm being really honest, this has crept into the realm of Oftentimes when it comes to my older sons—it means my sons are reading and writing, and I can actually sit down and join them. Of course there are wild cards; there are six of them, after all, and they rarely choose to do the same thing at the same time, unless it involves a trampoline and karate chopping a brother's face off.

So, most of the time, I have a rocky relationship with silence. And maybe there's another reason for that: I don't really know what to do with the silence anymore. Read? Catch up on endless housework? Sign folders I haven't signed in a month? Cook a complicated three-course meal? (Well, that one's easy: No thanks.)

If I had a moment of silence, right this minute, I'd probably just pass out from exhaustion.

Rainy Days With Twins: a Horror Story

It's been raining unusually often here in the grand state of Texas. Usually, by this time every summer, we're all parched and dying of heat stroke, the grass so brown it's hard to tell if it's actually grass or an extra-fluffy layer of dirt.

Maybe it's just my imagination, but it seems like, with the world looking so green, it's marginally easier to handle my six sons at home for the summer break with a measure of patience. And while I'm thankful for the rain and all this green and the slightly lower temperatures, I have to admit: rain is getting to be an inconvenience.

Mainly because my sons don't get to go outside.

I have no problem with my sons playing in the rain. In fact, I recently encouraged them to get out in their swimsuits and dance. The problem is really what they find to do in the rain, which generally boils down to one simple variable: mud.

The other day one of my twins came in looking like a walking mud pile, even though I'd specifically told him to stay out of the mud, so I've temporarily revoked the rain-dancing privileges, and now we get to be a cozy family cooped up inside.

My older sons are really good at finding something to do—

reading stories, writing poetry, creating art, building with LEGO pieces. But my twins are masters of deception and will wait until Husband or I am distracted by some other crisis (and there are many in our home) to have their way with... well, pretty much anything.

These two are the wildest balls of energy, and as such, are probably the most exhausting children of mine to watch and protect and, mainly, keep out of things about which they've already been warned.

By the end of a rainy day, I am wishing, wishing, wishing I could send them outside.

Here's what happens when my twins don't get enough outdoor time:

They close themselves in the bathroom without my noticing, and, very quietly, they take three toilet paper rolls (the expensive, eco-friendly kind), shove them in the toilet, and then flush, just to "see what happens."

They find some random chalk somewhere—who knows where, someone's got a stockpile, apparently—and they mark up their walls with cave paintings that they'll deny until they're red in the face, because they don't want to clean it all up. And then they'll have way too much fun cleaning it up with wet rags.

They take down every shirt in their closet and try them on. They come to dinner wearing fourteen shirts each.

They aggravate their brothers, following them around, picking up their Pokémon cards without permission, trying to read over their shoulders (who likes people reading over their shoulder? I can completely understand the complaint on this one, though my older sons don't remember their preferences when it's my shoulder over which they're reading) and then complain when a brother smacks them for their aggravating.

They steal important papers and mark on them with a permanent marker someone left out (it was probably me, because I thought we were past the permanent-marker-marking-spree stage) and now I not only can't tell how much this bill was but I also don't know who it's from.

They rearrange the shoes in all the baskets, mixing up matches, because they're trying to help (and they like stinky things).

They fill up with water the balloons they got at a party and think it's okay to throw them at each other in the house (has it ever been okay, sons? No. Now mop it all up with a towel, which is, no, not your hair.)

They take the slap bracelets they also got at a party and try to see if they work on their penises (What the—). Those slap bracelets are now in the trash. Forever and always.

They stash LEGO pieces under their bed so they'll have something to play with during nap time (the dead giveaway is how little they protest about nap time).

They break all the crayons in half because "it's fun." And then they complain about how they have no supplies with which to color anymore. Natural consequences. They aren't getting more crayons for a while. The stubs will have to do.

They take all the lids off the markers and leave them off because they "forgot." So the markers dry up. And they complain about not having any more markers. They now have no crayons (at least not any whole ones) and no markers, and I'm the meanest mom in the whole world and they hate me because I won't buy them more.

They rip out all the pages of their brothers' new notebooks and call it a lovely day (it certainly is, isn't it? Look at that rain! Now go play outside!).

They sneak into the candy stash they picked up at the same birthday party where they got the balloons and the slap bracelets, and they try to pretend they didn't eat anything, even though wrappers litter the floor, one of them has blue fingers (from the blow pop he completely destroyed), and the other has a chocola-stache.

They jump on the couches like they're trampolines, because they haven't had adequate time on the real trampoline today.

They get a wild hair while I'm in the bathroom for maybe a little longer than I should be and decide they'd like to play in the rain. They put on twelve layers of clothes, because it's cold out there in the wet world. Once they realize this wasn't the best idea, they come back in dripping. With twelve layers of clothes. Which I will have to immediately put in the dryer, even though today was not laundry day. As I'm walking to the dryer, I'll slip in the puddles they left me on the floor, and, as though I weren't already black and blue by the time this rainy day is over, I'll have another souvenir on my backside, because not everyone is great at falling, okay?

They eat. And eat. And eat. They'll eat us out of house and

home on a rainy day. I don't even have anything left to fix for dinner, because they decided they'd also eat the salad when everything else was gone.

They decorate a whole table with almonds, and, when trying to pick them all up, sweep most of them onto the floor. I think it was a ploy to also eat all the almonds.

They destroy a toilet (because of the above).

They open the door to see if it's still raining, and they forget to close it, which means twelve thousand flies (which are still out in the rain—how?) come darting in, because ours is the best house on the block for fly nourishment.

They break into the garage Husband and I are trying to clean out and undo in five minutes our hours of hard work.

They go scavenging for treasures in the cushions of the couches and find all kinds of old toys I thought we'd effectively given away. Toys are always coming back. I have no idea why they like this house so much.

They whine incessantly about wanting to play outside (quickly forgetting how they already tried).

Sanity is important for parenting. My days consist of multiple times when I will send my sons outside—not only because I need them to shake off a little energy but also because outdoor time is good for them. With the rain, we're all stuck inside. Together. Like a happy little family that's getting way too close for anyone's comfort.

I love rain. But I could really use some sunshine right about now.

When the Dramatic Kid Hits a Wall

My kid's face was a scraped-up mess—but you should've seen the wall.

There wasn't a mark on it.

We were happily bathing our younger sons, trying to keep the fifteen gallons of water inside the tub for once, when our nine-year-old came into the house howling. Now, this isn't all that unusual in my house, as you might imagine—not with six sons. This particular son has a penchant for being…dramatic. For example, one day we were at a local museum, which has a kids' area with kid-sized workout equipment, and he was adjusting the seat on the stationary bike and accidentally scratched his leg on a pedal. He fell to the floor like he was dying, moaning so loudly and persistently that a museum worker came over to us and asked if he needed some ice or a first-aid kit or maybe an ambulance. There was hardly a scratch on him. I thanked her for her concern and told her he'd be just fine, and, sure enough, thirty seconds later, he was chasing after one of his brothers who had accidentally picked up the book the then-eight-year-old had brought with him, because he brings books everywhere, in case there's a second or two between exhibits when he'll have a chance to bury himself in a sentence.

He comes howling into the house when he's tried "skating" with two scooters, one on each foot, and runs into the van. He comes howling into the house when his brother mis-aims a ball and hits him on the foot. He comes howling into the house when he jumps off the trampoline the wrong way (and yet still does it again).

So, of course, we didn't think much of this little display, since the boy has cried wolf multiple times, and, to reiterate, we were in the middle of bathing his brothers.

My son limped up the stairs and into the bathroom, and this time we knew it was for real. His chin was bleeding, his upper lip was bleeding, and his knee was smeared with red.

"What in the world happened?" I said, freaking out a little but trying hard not to show it. I've learned my sons gauge what their response should be by judging my response—particularly the eyes.

"I ran into the front of the house," he said.

"How did you do that?" Husband said.

"I was riding my scooter too fast and couldn't stop when I came around the corner of the house," my son said.

Husband and I looked at each other in the way all couples do when they're trying not to laugh at their kid (don't you know it makes it worse to look at each other? Stop it!). I averted my eyes and coughed. I could visualize it completely: the way he was cruising down the cul-de-sac, how cocky he gets about his scooter "skillz," how his face might have looked when he realized he'd misjudged the timing and the wall was coming at him much faster than he'd intended—it really wasn't funny. It wasn't. Stop laughing.

Sometimes having a vivid visual imagination is a curse.

Husband and I checked him over for broken bones and doctored up his scrapes, listening to him talk about how he wouldn't be able to walk to school tomorrow and probably couldn't even go at all because he was so beat up. And you know what? I almost felt sorry enough for him to say he could stay home (he's very good at generating a yes). Except he's nine. If I'd done what he did, I would be in the hospital for a week. But he's nine. His body is much more capable of bouncing right back.

So I smiled at him and said, "I hope you've learned your lesson, sweet boy."

What lesson would that be? Well, apparently he didn't know, either. Three minutes later, he was back out on the scooter, trying to race his brothers down the hill, darting at an impossible speed between the van's front bumper and the wall that had beat him up, just so he could be the first one inside and win the prize of…

Nothing.

Glitter, Glitter, Everywhere; Clean it Up: It's Still There!

"One day, baby," Husband said.

"One day what?" I said, because usually this ends with something dream-like, as in "One day we'll go to Paris" or "One day we'll take a weekend to New York" or "One day we'll have a clean house," but it was too early in the morning for dreaming big like that.

"One day we'll be able to walk around our house and not get glitter on us," Husband said.

I'd say that's just as big a dream as the others.

I'm not entirely sure where our house picked up glitter. I have some stuffed away in a Hobby Lobby bag that we take out once a year for decorating Christmas ornaments. As far as I know, my sons don't know about it.

What I do know for sure is that the other day, Husband and I left our older sons downstairs for their Quiet Time, which is a time in our house, usually from noon to 3 p.m. that we set aside for creating or reading or doing some kind of quiet activity, while those who need to take a nap can sleep without interruption.

These sons are getting older and don't need quite as much supervision during their Quiet Time (or so we thought), so this particular day Husband and I decided to take a power nap and get a little work done after the nap. We gave them explicit instructions, along with a list of permitted activities. Crafting with glitter was not on the list.

An hour later, when we returned back downstairs to check on them, green glitter was all over the dining room table, in neat little piles. "I'm going to use it," my seven-year-old said, probably an involuntary response to the horrified look on my face.

"Where'd you get it?" I said.

He shrugged. "In the art cabinet."

I eyed the glitter piles and shook my head. "Just don't let it get everywhere," I said. Before turning away, I eyed those glitter piles again, like I could somehow convince them to stay exactly where they were.

But everyone who knows glitter knows that glitter has no boundaries.

Now that green glitter is everywhere.

There are specks on faces, in mouths, inside ears, all over pants. That night, we had glitter in our chicken soup, glitter in our water, glitter in our spice cookies for dessert.

There is glitter on my laptop. There is glitter on all our books. There is glitter on the seat of my pants and on every surface of my sons' skin.

It's now been weeks. It doesn't matter how many times Husband or I have wiped up that glitter and thrown it in the trash. Glitter is more persistent than our sticky-brained nine-year-old. It is never going away. It will never relent.

"Hey, Mama, come look at my poop!" said my five-year-old today. This is not such an unusual request in a household of boys, so I fell for the trap.

His poop winked at me, it had so much glitter in it.

I'm starting to think I'm in a creepy movie that sparkles. I'm not quite sure how I'm supposed to get out of it.

The Unending Challenges of Laundry

I usually tackle at least eight loads of laundry every Tuesday—and that's if my sons don't decide to put in the laundry all the clean clothes living on their floor, instead of making the effort to hang them up. Which they did this week, after Husband and I helped them clean their atrocious room and found six weeks' worth of clothes on the floor.

We couldn't tell if they were clean or dirty, so in the hamper they went.

On weeks like this, I'll gain an extra load or two.

There are three steps to Laundry Day in my house. Some of those steps get more attention than others.

Step One: Washing and Drying

It takes me all day to do laundry, because I don't own a laundromat. And then it takes at least forty-five minutes to sort all that laundry.

I know, I know. My sons should be helping. And they will, eventually. It's just that I usually only get to laundry when they're in school, because when they're home I'm so busy mediating fights and keeping them out of the refrigerator that I can't possibly juggle laundry in addition to all that. I'm easily overstimulated. What can I say?

Also, I would kind of like to have my laundry done and not stalled out, which happens often when my sons are invited into the laundry process. Mostly because we have heavy-duty machines with a billion buttons, and if we know anything at all about kids, we know they like pressing buttons. So sometimes the towels get washed on the delicate cycle in boiling hot water with enough water for a "tiny load" instead of the "gigantic load" it actually is.

Sometimes, if I'm really lucky on this laundry day, the washer won't even be washing like I think it is, and I won't know until my phone timer clangs, telling me the load is done and I find that it is not, in fact, done, because someone pushed the start button one extra time, and it never got past the soaking stage, which just, essentially, added an hour to my laundry day.

My kids give the best gifts.

So I just do laundry myself, for now.

Step Two: Sorting and Folding

The way I fold laundry is I first dump it all out on my bed and then sort it into its eight different piles. Actually seven; we combine our twins' clothes, because I can't tell what is whose and I'll leave them to duke it out.

Why do I fold on my bed? you may be asking. It's a clever reason, if I do say so myself: If the piles are blocking my bed, that means we can't go to sleep until they're put away. Husband, who is charged with the responsibility of teaching our sons to put away their laundry, because I've just spent an entire day washing it, doesn't feel the same way I do, though.

The piles are just mountains to be moved. Where is a good second home for these mountains? The banister outside our bedroom door.

Step Three: Putting Laundry Away

We're busy people. Most people are busy people. Husband and I are both entrepreneurs. We work in creative fields, which are, if anything, inconsistent fields. I'm extremely consistent in my writing practices, but even I don't know when that irresistible creative urge—the one that says, "Sit down right this minute and write this down"—will hit me.

And then there are six kids on top of our careers.

So those piles on the banister outside our bedroom door stay piles for a long while. Actually, that's not true. They don't stay piles at all.

Here's what the breakdown usually looks like:

A boy approaches while I'm standing at the stove frying eggs for their breakfast. I haven't woken them yet, because boys are bears without the promise of food first thing in the morning. This one woke early. "Mama, I don't have any sweat pants in my drawer," he'll say.

"Okay," I'll say. "You probably have some in your laundry pile. I'll come help you find them in a minute."

"Okay," he'll say, like he understands. He'll disappear. I know what he's doing, but I am powerless to stop it.

While I finish up breakfast, get the plates on the table, set the youngest in his high chair, he yells from upstairs: "Don't worry, Mama! I got some."

I can feel the physical deflation.

I deflate because I know what the floor outside my bedroom is going to look like when I venture back upstairs. Apparently, every single time we do laundry, the sweat pants, which are the only pants my sons deem worth wearing anymore, are always at the very bottom of the pile. Which means those sorted laundry piles don't remain sorted laundry piles. They have crossed the line into Laundry Explosions that look frightfully similar to the one that happened the day I fell down the stairs carrying the laundry basket and broke my left foot.

We've gotten so used to walking on clothes (I'm not even sure we have a real floor anymore) that I don't know what we're going to do when someone decides to clean this up.

Mom's Night Out: Totally Worth the Atrocious Mess

I'm part of a monthly book club, because I like to read and I love getting together with a small group of women to chat about books and dreams and husbands. But mostly life.

My group meets once a month. We sit on couches and stuff ourselves with desserts and drink wine and talk and laugh and remember what it's like to be more than Wife and Mom.

Husband and my sons know when it's time for my book club meeting, because I'm typically in the kitchen trying to top those dark chocolate brownies with the dark chocolate buttercream icing I just whipped up in a bowl (because desserts are better from scratch). They'll saunter in and beg for tastes and follow up the request with, "Will there be some left for us?"

Well, that depends on how the week has gone for the ladies.

My book club friends and I meet late enough in the evening where I can help with after-dinner chores and bathing my sons and even starting their evening story time so Husband isn't completely overwhelmed with putting six boys to bed (it takes multiple people to do a good job. Probably more than two, which means most of the time Husband and I are barely getting by with "good job." We call it "good enough job.").

But sometimes my pumpkin sugar cookie experiment doesn't turn out quite the way I wanted it to (shocking, since I don't really use recipes, I just dump ingredients together; most of the time they turn out fine, because baking is one of my strengths—fortunately or unfortunately, however you want to look at that). When this happens, I have to take a quick trip to the store for some chocolate candy or cupcakes or someone else's brownies. For this, I'll leave right after dinner, which means Husband has to execute the after-dinner chores six-on-one. He always says he'll be just fine. That's because he doesn't actually make them do their chores. He sends them out to play instead, while he listens to a podcast and rinses all the dishes and forgets to start the dishwasher.

When I return home way past my bedtime, I never peek at the kitchen, because it's dark and I'm terribly afraid of the dark. So it's not until I rise the next morning and enter the kitchen so I can fix my sons' breakfast that I notice the atrocious mess.

Why are yesterday's onions still sitting in that bowl, on top of the cutting board on which he sliced them last night, like they didn't even move? Answer: Because no one I know would touch after-dinner chores with six young boys and only one parent home to referee what will likely happen, which is this: sword fighting with the broom and the mop, wet rags flying across the kitchen, spray bottles of homemade cleaner soaking backs with vinegar. And that's just getting started.

I completely understand. I don't like the messy kitchen greeting me when I wake up on that one Friday morning a month, but what am I going to do? Certainly not stay home. I deserve this night out.

I've been attending this book club for more than two years now. I have returned home at 11 p.m. to find Husband playing some songs to friends on social media and an eight-year-old still reading upstairs in the library because someone forgot to tell him it was time for lights out. I have returned to the four-year-old twins dressed in their seventeen-month-old brother's pajamas (it's not even spandex. It's a second skin with dinosaurs etched into it) because someone didn't check to make sure they weren't tearing their room apart by unfolding all the folded clothes. I have returned to a six-year-old curled up on the floor outside our bedroom and Husband inside watching a movie with headphones he said blocked out the knocks on the door (there are so many!).

It's not that Husband can't handle six boys. He was a boy himself once; he's generally better at it than I am. We just do things differently, that's all.

So when I'm done shaking my head about how that rock-hard piece of bread possibly made it past the eyes of the parent on duty who wasn't me and into the top bunk of a four-year-old, where it was flattened and broken by his thrashing body and distributed liberally throughout the room during the night, I usually just thank Husband for understanding and supporting my need to escape the house every now and then.

Cleaning up a toilet-papered bathroom is totally worth taking a mom's night out. Every single time.

A Little Shop of Horrors in My Very Own House

Words I never want to hear again: "It's a haunted house, Mama! We even made bloody fingers for snacks!"

Herein lies the problem with parenting an entrepreneurial nine-year-old: the ideas fly fast—much faster than the logic. In fact, logic can't even hope to keep up.

Some days I come down the stairs to billions of drawings he wants to set up outside so he can sell them to the neighbors for five dollars. Some days I come down the stairs to old boxes cut into pet homes that he'd like to take out front and sell as, that's right, pet homes. Today I came down the stairs to a little shop of horrors.

It was remarkable, in a way. I hadn't left them alone for more than five or ten minutes, and by the time I returned from holing away in the bathroom (it's my only respite), what they'd envisioned—a haunted house—had become reality in record time.

On my dining room table were plates of bloody fingers. They weren't really fingers, of course—though they could have been, considering my sons had unauthorized use of knives while I was hiding away (I should have known when the house turned quiet). They had cut up bananas, which their imagination identified as the closest thing to fingers they could find. On top of those chopped bananas (which were actually several inches longer than my fingers), they had draped honey, jam, and peanut butter. Yum.

This delightful snack was provided for the people who "visit our haunted house," my sons told me—because they're good at hospitality when they want to be. There were six plates of these bloody fingers. I couldn't look at them without gagging. I know it was only strawberry jam, but still.

Another feature of this haunted house was…an obstacle course? A wannabe tent? A seating area that isn't really a seating area? I didn't get what they were trying to do; I only really saw the destruction of my entire living room. They explained that "people will crawl through this and we'll be waiting on the other side to scare them." It didn't seem all that scary, except the first time you looked at it. Disasters are a little jarring, especially the ones in your own house.

I thought maybe I had to try it to understand its scary factor, so I wriggled my way into the obstacle course (I think that's what I finally decided it should be called). They didn't scare me; all they really did was giggle the whole time, because I could hardly get my butt through the legs of the overturned piano bench (it's really small). The scariest part of the whole thing was considering how I would possibly explain to Husband that I needed help peeling a piano bench off my backside.

In the kitchen my sons showed me "the room where ghosts knocked down all the chairs." Which I suppose *could* be pretty freaky, especially if those ghosts are kids. Specifically identical twins. Remember those girls in *The Shining?* Kids are the creepiest. (Also, I'm pretty sure the bloody fingers must have dropped on the kitchen floor at some point during the production line, because there were splatters caked beside one of the chairs. At least I hope that's what it was. I don't think I want to know otherwise.)

In the downstairs bathroom, they showed me the "haunting minion," which was only a small little minion toy. I almost laughed at their "it's so scary, isn't it" until they turned off the bathroom lights and shut the door and the toy started talking. This toy has never talked. I mean, it did, but its batteries ran out months ago, and I learned a long time ago that I should never replace the batteries in any battery-powered toy if I wanted to keep my sanity, which is paramount as a parent.

My sons almost had to pull me off the floor after that.

I love how creative my sons can be. I love that their little amazing minds imagined and executed something as elaborate as this haunted house (which they said they'd charge everyone a dollar to pass through, which I think might be a little high), but we had to close up the little shop of horrors soon after they took me on their tour, because it was time for dinner and we needed all the overturned chairs. They were disappointed they didn't make any money off their efforts, but I explained to them that there are easier ways to make money that don't require so much setup for very little payoff. They weren't interested in hearing about it; they were already planning their next haunted house. Tomorrow.

When Kids Discover the Entertainment of Spit Balls

We don't get many guests at our house anymore. I tell myself it's not because of our downstairs bathroom, which is the one guests are encouraged to use. But some days I don't believe myself.

It's not just that this bathroom smells like a swamp. It's also that there is always mud streaking the sink, from boys playing out back in the pit I told them to "stay away from or else" and, of course, they thought they'd experiment and see what "or else" meant (which was pretty much nothing), after which they trampled inside to wash their hands (some didn't bother with that part of it). It's also that there are soggy toilet paper rolls drying in the trash can, because one of the four-year-old twins decided it would be hilarious to stick one in the sink and flip on the water and watch it "turn curly." At least this is what we hope he did. Nothing has been confirmed, because when you ask a four-year-old "What happened?" you're likely to hear all about a roly poly out in the backyard that he put into the cracks between the porch rails and how he fell on his booty but it didn't hurt and then he ate some popcorn that I didn't make today but which he probably found tucked into the couch from the last movie night three weeks ago. All things considered, even though the story didn't match the question, I'd rather assume it's not potty water soaking that toilet paper roll and the floor and his white monster shirt (which is not so white anymore) that he refused to take off because "I LOVE THIS MONSTER AND HE NEEDS ME TO WEAR HIM AND HE'S MY FRIEND AND I DON'T CARE IF MY SHIRT IS WET." I didn't feel like arguing for thirty-six hours, so I let it be. The soaked shirt is drying on the four-year-old's torso.

It's also that there are gigantic spit balls leering at me from the ceiling every time I dare to think I might use this bathroom instead of climbing up all those steps to my no-boys-allowed one.

This bathroom is supposed to be our best foot forward—the one we make pristine and sanitary (at the very least) for our guests. I am always, always embarrassed when someone's visiting and they say, "Where's your bathroom?" and I want so badly to say, "We don't have one" but I know how that would come across. I always want to give a disclaimer or some kind of warning that will encompass everything that has happened in this bathroom. It doesn't matter how many times Husband cleans it (he's assigned to this task because I have a sensitive gag reflex and boys are not currently great at aiming their excrement). It doesn't matter how recently that cleaning happened. It doesn't matter if none of my sons have even used it since that cleaning. They have left their marks everywhere. Most notably, now, on the ceiling.

We're not really sure which of our sons executed this spit-balls-on-the-ceiling prank. We're only sure that the giant balls have been there for three weeks now, because Husband and I are too exhausted to scrape them off the ceiling (also: who wants to touch that?).

I'm sure it was so much fun. I can imagine one of them closing and locking himself in this bathroom under the guise of needing to "go number two," because he knew it would buy him some time. And it probably wasn't even premeditated. He was probably washing his hands and looked down at the toilet paper roll dripping in the trash can and then, innocently enough, looked up at the ceiling. Then back at the soggy roll and back at the ceiling and start it all over again while wheels began turning in his oh-so-creative brain. What would happen when wet toilet paper met a dry ceiling? He might have torn off a small piece of that soggy toilet paper and tossed it up with all the force his little six-year-old body could manage, just to see if it would stick. And it did. And then he realized this could be a fun game, and he waved his older brothers into the bathroom and they all started playing "How Big Can We Make a Spitball That Sticks to the Ceiling."

And before we even knew what was happening, we had a ceiling full of gigantic spit balls.

I remember the endless games of spitballs when I was a kid. My brother would stuff bigger and bigger wads of wet paper into a straw and launch them toward our ceiling. Boys at school would do it while the teacher's back was turned, and the boys with the biggest wads that stuck and went unnoticed by the teacher got the most points.

I never did understand its entertainment merit. It just

made me shudder a little, walking under all that spit. Maybe that was the point.

My brother and the boys at school never got such an impressive wad of toilet paper to stick to a ceiling. I've been researching the biggest spit ball record in the Guinness Book of World Records. I'm pretty sure my kids are close to beating it.

What Happens the Week Before a Kidless Weekend

"Enjoy it. It goes so fast."

We hear these words so often. In grocery stores, out in our city, in our own families.

And yes. They're right. It does go fast. You have your baby one day, and the next day he's running away from you in the park. You try to get your kid to eat some mushed-up carrots one day and the next day he's stealing thirty from the crisper drawer, grinning at you like he's innocent. You walk your kid to school one day, and the next day he's driving himself.

Just yesterday I was holding my oldest son in my arms, and today he's nine. How did he suddenly get those knobby-kneed legs and a smart(er) mouth and a running speed that makes me work as hard as I can to not completely embarrass myself when we're racing up the street because he's really good at the flight response when anything doesn't go his way? (He doesn't know we're racing, but we totally are. Also, he's not really running away. He just needs a little movement sometimes, to get all the confusing steam out of his body. He knows where he's loved most, and he'll always come back. I just like to get a little exercise and make sure he doesn't get run over by the neighborhood drivers trying to navigate by iPhone.)

In other words, I'm very familiar with the time-flying thing. I see and marvel at it practically every day.

However. This weekend Husband and I get to have a rare kid-less weekend. It's the first time this year that we've had the opportunity to spend three consecutive days without all the kids (thanks, Mom!). I'm sure we'll have to usher our kids through Grandparent Detox, but those three days are worth it every time.

I'm counting down the days until we are free.

Which means, of course, the days are crawling.

I've lived enough hours for it to be Friday already. Except it's not. It's still Monday afternoon.

This morning Husband and I bolted out of our beds at 3 because there was a seal in our house. We followed the seal's bark to our twins' room, where one was still sleeping and the other was wide awake, and discovered the noise did not, in fact, belong to a seal and would not have, under any circumstances, belonged to a seal because this is Texas (try telling that to a mind that hasn't quite woken yet from dreams that are most often strange and fantastical). The sound belonged to the five-year-old.

So we got to have a little 3 a.m. party in the twins' room, where we gave him a breathing treatment from the breathing apparatus we procured when he was an infant with RSV. No one really went back to sleep after that.

An hour and a half later, my alarm gently told me it was time to get up. I generally do some writing in the morning and some reading and a workout. But because my twins were already awake and running circles, so it seemed, in their room, I did none of these things. I sat and stared into space, thinking about how many more days until I could sleep without an ear tuned to my sleeping—or no longer sleeping—children.

Sometimes a mom just needs a break.

Then the morning rush started. The eight-year-old couldn't find his shoes, the seven-year-old had no clean socks, the five-year-olds had no folders signed and were supposed to read a book to us last night and didn't, would you like to hear it now? We walked everyone but the seal to school—some later than others—and returned to the house just so I could tell the sick five-year-old minute after minute after minute: "Don't touch that. It's your brother's."

Nap time lasted fifteen minutes, two toilets overflowed, Lightning McQueen caused a fistfight, the plunger saw some unsupervised action, and my mantra became, "Four more days. Four more days. Four more days."

Just four more days. How bad could it be?

I shouldn't have asked.

By the time Friday rolled around, we had six more plunger incidents, hieroglyphics on closet walls, fourteen more hours searching for shoes, three pounds of strawberries consumed in one sitting (by one boy), twelve LEGO creations destroyed beyond recognition (by twins, of course), two plants give up on the hands that rocked them, and a kid who had cut his bangs in an unfortunate way.

Freedom always comes with a price. But at least the price comes with freedom.

How Often Do Children Fight? Every Other Minute

With so many children in my house (and home for the summer!), it seems like there's a fight every other minute. Research has proven that children fight three and a half times every hour—which, I suspect, seems like every other minute to their parents.

While research tells me this is quite normal, it still doesn't calm my fraying nerves.

Some fights, of course, are more important than others. Sometimes a kid swipes a toy from another kid, sometimes they're arguing over a memory, sometimes they are genuinely trying to work out their feelings and arguing is the only way they can do it.

Sometimes they argue just to argue.

Here are some of the most ridiculous things my kids argue about:

1. How many snacks their brothers have had.

Husband and I don't let our sons have multiple snacks every day. They have to wait until 3 p.m. for the first and only snack, because we eat breakfast, lunch, and dinner at specified times, together, with a large array of food. Snacking all the time means my kids likely wouldn't eat one of those three meals, which means I wasted half an hour (or more) cooking and preparing it. I don't like wasted time, so we remedy this with one snack time a day.

When 3 p.m. rolls around, my older sons get two snacks and my younger ones get one.

The problem is that once Husband or I get started on dinner, our attention lags a little. And that's when my sons start raiding the fridge. If one brother gets an extra snack, another brother wants an extra snack. They start fighting about who had what, how unfair it is, and how terrible this household is because they're all starving to death.

It's one of my favorite fights ever.

2. Who's going to use the dish wand first.

When my sons finish eating, they are expected to wash out whatever bowls or plates they use. It's a shame there's only one dish wand. That means when boys finish their snacks at the same time—or, when they're in school, they all get home at the same time—they will fight to the death about who gets the dish wand first. I should probably save myself the trouble and just get a couple extra dish wands, but what can I say? I like torturing myself.

Chores also see this delightful little argument, usually because we only have one rag with which to wipe both the counters and the table (which are two separate chores for two separate sons). Who's going to do their chore first? Depends on who's fastest or strongest.

3. What color their shirt is.

Is it red or maroon, or maybe brick red? This fight can

sometimes last up to twenty minutes. Every time I think they've resolved it, someone else will throw out another color (thank you, Crayola, for your thousand different ways to say red), and it will start all over again. This fight will evolve into which shade of red is the best, who has the better color judgment, and who knew their colors best at the youngest age.

What does it matter? They don't care. They just want to fight.

4. Who put the shoes where.

If my sons are exceptional at one thing (they're exceptional at more, but they're *really* exceptional at this), it's blaming. They will blame until they're blue in the face (and they'll blame someone else for turning their face blue!). The most frequent place this blaming can be witnessed is when they're trying to find their shoes.

They put their shoes where they belong, they say. Their brothers must have moved them.

I know, however, that all of them left their shoes out by the trampoline yesterday, because, even though we reminded them to bring all the shoes inside, they were too tired after jumping for so long. When they shockingly find their shoes out by the trampoline like I said, they will point fingers about which brother is responsible for five pairs of shoes sitting outside. It certainly was not them.

5. Whose LEGO piece it is.

All my sons get different LEGO sets for their birthdays, and they will try their hardest to keep them separated. But, alas, LEGOs like each other, and it's impossible to keep sets separate, at least in my house. And, also, the pieces for individual sets look mostly the same, with a few exceptions. So when one is holding up a plain yellow LEGO piece, and another sees it and says it's his, they will fight about it for hours, even though both their sets came with a yellow piece exactly like this one.

I don't know how they know which is whose, but they believe they do. And they will not rest until they convince their brother it's true (which will be never, by the way; persistence runs in my family).

6. Who turned the light on.

The rule in our house is if no one is in a room, the light must be turned off. When I mention this about forty times a day, my sons will fight over who turned the light on, unaware that this is not necessary information to have. When I remind them that the responsibility for turning off a light lies on the last one who left the room, they will fight about that, too. The one who is first in the room is the one who should turn it off, they say—he's the one who turned it on in the first place, after all.

I'll remind them of that when they're in the middle of peeing and their brother, who was the first one in the bathroom, turns the light off mid-stream.

7. Which vitamins are better—dark or light.

Our vitamins come in two different shades: light mauve and dark mauve. Somehow my sons have gotten it in their heads that the dark ones mean they're "bad" and the light ones mean they're "good". We don't even use this language—"good" and "bad" people; we say "people who make good and bad decisions"—around our house, but their imaginations have conjured up all sorts of ridiculous realities.

If, in the random doling out of vitamins, one boy gets two dark vitamins, he will cry like the world is ending because he doesn't want to be "bad." He will ask a brother to trade, and thus ensues yet another fight.

I think it's time to change vitamins.

8. Who gets to sit next to the baby.

Every time we sit down to eat, my sons will fight over who gets to sit next to the youngest. At home, we have assigned seating, which makes this particular fight easier, but out at restaurants or when we're eating dinner at church or at the grandparents' house, or, basically, anywhere that is not home, this fight happens with such regularity I can almost time it.

I, of course, need to sit by the youngest in case he chokes while he's eating. But that other place? Everyone wants it every time. They don't realize that what usually happens during the course of a dinner is that the youngest will turn to them with his messy fingers and try to touch them. They've even been the grossed-out victims of this. It doesn't matter. They still fight over that coveted place. I guess I should be glad they love their baby brother, but mercy. Stop fighting.

9. Who is responsible for that awful smell.

This is not the kind of fight you'd expect (or maybe it is). Rather than blame the awful smell on someone else, my sons will all willingly take the blame for this one. They are incredibly proud of the smells discharged from their feet, their mouths, or their rear ends, and they will fight over who was responsible for that last one, which, if its odor cloud had a color, would be a perfect blend of green and brown. Chartreuse, I believe they call it.

The best thing about boys and their constant arguing is that the emotional side of arguing is over almost before it begins. Boys don't hold any grudges or keep their hurt feelings balled up inside—at least not usually. One minute they're ready to pound each other's faces, the next minute they're tripping each other on the floor for a lively game of "Who Can Stand the Longest."

Which means I have a few minutes to recover before the next fight breaks out. Exactly what I need to pop a few dark chocolate squares without the scavengers noticing.

It's the little things.

THE PADDED WALLS OF PARENTHOOD

When You Practice Gratitude at Your Dinner Table

Dinnertime's a mess.

Not only are there kids complaining about what we're having for dinner (because that's one thing you can always count on with children, unless you make every night Pizza Night, which is not good for my figure—but hey, neither were children), burping at persistent intervals, and wiping their noses on each other (if you're the twins), but everyone is also trying to talk all over each other in an imaginary race to get Husband's and my attention and be the first to deliver the news of the day.

Because of this madness, Husband and I have allocated part of dinner time for reviewing thankfuls. This is a time, usually right after dinner is served because you can't count on attentiveness for long, unless my sons have food in front of them, when we ask each child to share anything for which they are thankful.

We get the attention of our children, who should be familiar with this routine, since it's been going on for more than six years, by yelling into the fray: "It's time to do our thankfuls!" in a way that sounds like we're not really thankful at all.

It's just the noise. There's always so much noise. I have no idea how people can make so much noise when they're eating. My sons are masters at it.

Plus, by the end of the day, I can feel my whole attitude shifting downward with spiraling momentum; I'm an introvert living in a house of seven males, and by the time dinner rolls around I'm ready for some silent reading in my bedroom with the door closed.

Which means I also need these thankfuls.

Leading our sons in this thankfulness practice has many benefits. It teaches our sons how to take turns talking, which is something even the nine-year-old still forgets (he has the most words to say, according to him. And he might be right). It teaches us to focus on the good, which has lasting effects on attitude and mindset. It helps us recognize how fortunate we really are—to be together, to be eating as a family, to be alive.

The problem is that my children are thankful for things like twenty French fries instead of only ten, and after one kid has listed the billion foods that exist in the world that make him feel thankful for being alive, my eye starts twitching. The clock's counting down the minutes before dinner is over, and we've only made it through one child. We have five more to go, plus Husband and me. We'll be here until tomorrow morning.

And then I realize, with a jolt—this is gratitude. He—the kid who won't shut up—is teaching me gratitude. Gratitude for French fries and pizza and the salad that sustains us when it's Mama's turn to cook dinner.

Though it seems trite and unimportant sometimes, my

If These Walls Could Talk

children are sharing the things that are close to their hearts, and who cares if they use a thousand words where I could say it in ten because they're more like their daddy than they are me? It's unfortunate in this instance, but better in others. Husband doesn't worry nearly as much as I do. He lets circumstances roll over him like a soothing wave of warm water and keeps right on walking. I'm thankful for *that*.

With this daily, imperfect, wordy practice, my children are focusing their attention on the things they love in their lives. This is something to celebrate, even if it takes us twenty minutes to move on to the next person. What kinds of kids automatically feel thankful for something so simple as "the toilet flushed without overflowing"? Kids who live in my house, that's who.

So I've learned to listen with (mostly) rapt attention.

Tonight's thankfuls were especially charming:

Kid 1:

He's thankful for soccer socks—and that Mama washed them (What? He noticed?)—that have a big hole in the big toe because he's worn them every day this week and all the other weeks. He's thankful for running shorts that he can wear every day, too, because he doesn't care about looking nice yet, and, bonus, he's always ready to take off running, at a moment's notice, which helps when he's playing Infected on the school playground. He's thankful, too, for running shoes, because they make him fly.

Kid 2:

He's thankful that he got a piece of gum from the good-behavior treasure chest today and that he got to chew it for five hours (I'm thankful, too, because I didn't have to hear him ask a dozen times to have a piece here at home, which is usually the case; he thinks I might forget every half hour that I already gave him one. I don't forget anything. Well, that's not really true. However, I'm also not thankful for this piece of gum he got at school, because earlier, when he was laughing, it flew out of his mouth and landed on the carpet, at the same exact time someone tripped and put a toe in it, grinding gum into fibers. We had to cut it out, and now our carpet has a nice hole in it. I am thankful, though, that it did not lodge in someone's hair. So. Mostly thankful.). He's thankful for the sugary snack he guilted his friend into giving him at lunch, which explains a lot, now that I think about it. He's also thankful for his baby brother, which is a no-brainer; he's the cutest baby brother in the whole world (those aren't my words, but I completely agree).

Kid 3:

He's thankful for Pokémon and the brilliant minds that created it. He's thankful that he has a billion cards, which he spreads all over the living room floor so he can show us which ones he got in his stocking last year (as if we don't know). He's thankful for a binder that holds them all, even though Husband and I know we'll be walking on a Pokémon carpet in no time at all.

Kids 4 & 5

They're thankful for their booties and their penises and their burps and toots. They're thankful for their boogers, especially the kind that feel really good coming out, because the strings reach all the way up to their brain, maybe (gag). They're especially thankful they were given the ability to clear a room in less than a second with a sly little smile and a smell that would kill a skunk.

Can you tell they're four?

Kid 6

This kid hasn't started talking in complete sentences yet, but I'm pretty sure he's mostly thankful for me.

By the time the thankfuls are all said and done, there's no more dinner time left, but I don't mind that so much, because what their tiny little thankfuls are teaching me, every day we sit and listen to them for the forty-five minutes we can keep boys in their seats, is that we can always find thanks in the little things. Like so: I could be burning my nose hair irreparably on a fume of gas expelled from the backside of a nine-year-old, instead of just feeling slightly nauseated. So I'll be thankful, right now, for an invisible gas cloud that doesn't turn into a nose that can no longer smell, and, consequently, a tongue that can no longer taste.

That's the kind of thankful that's genuine in a house of boys.

One Thing I Know About Kids: They're Always Hungry

It used to be "I love you." My sons used to say those words all the time, every time they saw me or thought of me or pointed to a picture of me. They would come and kiss me or lay their head on me or wrap their arms around me and whisper the words in my ear, and I would melt every time.

Or maybe that's just how my mind remembers those early years of parenthood. Whatever.

All I know is lately that uttered-most-often phrase that used to melt me has been replaced by another that melts me in a completely different way.

"I'm hungry" has now overtaken "I love you." And not just by a margin—by a whole volcanic landslide.

The other day we were leaving for the annual family Christmas party a whole four-and-a-half hours away, the contemplation of which was already ratcheting up my anxiety, because who in their right mind likes to be trapped with six smelly boys in a Honda Odyssey (however comfortable the vehicle may be) for four-and-a-half hours (one way!)?

When Husband and I woke that morning, we decided, in an effort to preserve the relative cleanliness of our kitchen for when we returned late that evening, to grab something at the store for breakfast. Sure, we could have risen at 5 a.m. on a Saturday to leave on time for a Christmas party four-and-a-half hours away so we could feed them breakfast in our kitchen and still have time to clean up, but we also wanted to arrive at our destination alive. And, honestly, we'd stayed up too late the night before catching up on the latest episodes of *Game of Thrones*. So it was in the interest of all that we slept an extra hour and a half.

Still, we were feeling a little testy, which is the usual hangover of Not Enough Sleep. So after we'd explained to our sons that we were going to pick something up for breakfast at the store and strapped them all in and turned on *The Red Badge of Courage*, because we're a nerdy family that enjoys audio books during long trips, and the firstborn called from the back seat, "Okay, I'm ready to eat now," when we weren't even out of the neighborhood yet, Husband and I looked at each other and tried hard to swallow our sarcasm. Sometimes it's much too large to swallow.

"Oh," Husband said. "Oh, you're ready to eat right now. Well, I'll see if I can stop at this tree and get you something, then."

The nine-year-old looked out the window. "But I thought we were going to eat." And then, when he realized we were still in the middle of nowhere, because it had been forty-eight seconds since we'd pulled out of the driveway, his panic infused an extra, "But I'm hungry!" just to make sure we knew and would take this into account when we considered our surroundings, which, to reiterate, were nothing but trees.

This orchestrated a series of complaints from everyone else in the car, which ranged from "I feel light-headed, I'm so hungry" to "Well, I guess we're never gonna eat. You lied."

My sons are a tad bit dramatic. They get this from their father.

To further exemplify the magnitude of their irrationality, I must say that my sons have never NOT been fed. But details like this don't matter to hungry children, because, in their panic of facing the possibility of a few extra minutes without food, they can't possibly look back on the track record of the last nine years or eight years or whatever it may be, when they've eaten three (mostly) balanced meals a day and even been permitted (bonus!) at least one snack. The only one who wasn't shrieking was the youngest, because he trusts Mama and Daddy more than the others, though he's only been alive for two years.

I pulled out the trump card. "Should I turn the story off?" I said.

The nine-year-old was quick to answer. "No," he said. "It's just that I'm hungry." His repeated phrase caused a maddening chorus of "Me too," all around.

"I'll see if I can pull over this H-E-B truck up ahead," Husband said. He was clearly testier than I was. "Maybe they'll give us a sandwich."

I shot him a warning look. We'd just gotten them calmed down. I didn't want the shrieking to return. I said, "There are no stores around right this second. We can't stop until we get to a store. But don't worry. We're going to feed you."

"But I'm hungry!" the twins whined from just behind our seats. Apparently my words were not clear enough.

I tried again. "We'll feed you as soon as we can. As soon as we can. As soon as we can." Sometimes repeating myself makes a difference. In this case, it didn't. They just shrieked, "We heard you!" at the exact same time in exactly the same tone. Surround sound.

Husband looked at me and shook his head, smiling. Our sons were quiet until we pulled into the store and Husband ventured inside and took longer than one second. And then, of course, their daddy was taking too long. He was never going to come out. They were never going to eat again. They were going to die of starvation. We were the worst parents ever.

I told them to count the cars in the parking lot, but that took all of three minutes, because no one else was out this early on a Saturday.

Finally, finally, finally Husband returned and saved the day. I guess they were too busy stuffing their faces with blueberry bagels to say thank you. They didn't say another word until after they'd finished their bagels, and that was only to say, "Is there anything else to eat?"

My sons are always hungry. There are six of them, and they aren't even teenagers, but they can inhale two dozen eggs in a single morning and punctuate the inhale with an "I'm still hungry." They can eat five pounds of chicken and not bat an eye. Two of them sneaking into the freezer while I'm otherwise occupied cleaning up the latest mess somebody "askidentally" made can eat a twelve-ounce bag of frozen broccoli and still go looking for more. The most opened door in my home is the refrigerator one. They're always looking for something else to stuff in their faces.

Well, there's nothing left, because the schools are still on holiday break. My sons have eaten me out of my grocery budget. I can actually see what color my pantry shelves are now, because they're empty. The only good thing about it is I gave the refrigerator its first scrub-cleaning the other day, because it was the barest it's ever been. There's nothing left in our freezer. I have no idea what we're going to have for dinner tonight. Looks like popcorn, some chia seeds, and…a handful of old edamame my sons won't touch once it reaches "leftover" status.

Thank God school starts back up tomorrow. I won't have to initiate an unplanned fast.

Oh, also, hey teenage years: Stay far away, please.

The Mementos Kids Leave to Remind Me They're Still Here

Nothing makes me realize how much I miss my sons while they're at school quite like a holiday or a bad weather day, a day when they get to wake up at 6 a.m., even though there's no school, and hang out with me. I'm not even being sarcastic (yet). They're really cool kids, and even though it's hard to handle the dynamic of six little ones all the time, I really do enjoy spending time with them. When they're home and not at school, they show me all the stories they're writing, they show me their impressive LEGO creations, and we get to read books together and talk about what we learned from the books and imagine what it's like to live the life of the protagonist.

I like seeing them walking around the house. I enjoy studying their changing faces, which have lost some of their baby look, observing the sharpening of their edges and the lengthening of their forms. I even take pleasure in hearing the refrigerator door open every other minute, for at least the first hour or so.

But, lest I miss them too much while they're gone on a regular day, they leave me constant reminders that they exist.

I've found their reminders in the refrigerator, where they stash their cups of milk they didn't finish this morning that will usually curdle before they remember they had a cup of milk in the first place, because as soon as they get home they'll pour another giant glass, without even considering the first, and then they'll wonder, innocently, why the milk is gone three days before the next grocery trip. It's all dispersed in open cups in the refrigerator that are starting to smell significantly.

They leave their reminders on the floor, where my feet will get tangled in the pajamas they stripped off and left where they fell while I was distracted trying to keep my twins out of their oldest brother's room and away from his stuffed animals, which means I didn't remind them to put those pajamas in the laundry. (It doesn't matter how many times I remind them to pick up their clothes off the floor—it's even part of their morning routine, and they have a checklist in their hands—their pajamas still litter the floor so the next time I'm rushing to keep one of the four-year-olds from swinging off the ceiling fan in his room, my foot-tangle will become my busted knee).

They leave their reminders out on the back porch, where they forgot their good tennis shoes, which are now baking in the sun and the Texas heat, and sometimes they'll leave their socks in those baking shoes, so by the time they're remembered and retrieved, the socks are tie-dyed and the shoes are muted. Not only that, but they leave their underwear out there, which I can't, for the life of me, possibly explain or justify. Who was on duty when this happened? (Probably me. I like to take bathroom breaks when all six of the boys are my responsibility.)

They leave their reminders on the stairs, where they

dropped an armful of stuffed animals on their way down, which will sit there, taunting me, until I kick them mostly out of the way and hope I don't trip and fall down the stairs again. They leave their reminders in the puzzle they took out and didn't clean up again but left in the corner of the room, right where the eleven-month-old could find it and wash every piece with his mouth. They leave their reminders on the couches, which they probably just mistook for their jacket hooks.

They leave their reminders on my bed, where they took off their underpants to change them, because, evidently, a boy needs to change his underpants every twelve hours, even if he put on a fresh pair the night before (I know I'll be glad for this when they hit adolescence). They leave their reminders on my bedroom floor, where they spread out all their school papers, looking for that drawing they did for their teacher this weekend (it wasn't there, but they didn't bother to clean up the evidence of their looking). They leave their reminders under my covers, where they put that stick they found on their way out the door, and they knew the only place their twin brothers wouldn't go was my bedroom, and what better hiding spot to put it than under my covers, where no one would find it?! Genius!

They leave their reminders on the counter, where they stack the books they were reading—especially the one that made them miss the caravan walk to school, because they didn't hear a thing until the house got eerily silent and they realized they'd been left behind. They leave their reminders on the kitchen table, where they forgot to put their plate away when they were done with their breakfast. They leave their reminders on the dining room table, where I'll find a coloring sheet they took out for drawing, which the four-year-olds will ruin while they're at school.

They leave their reminders stuffed in hallway corners and pinned on walls and marinating in the toilet.

And you know what? I'm glad, because one day they'll be gone for good.

I'll take the reminders wherever I can find them. Fortunately, I don't have to look too hard.

(P.S. Boys, next time you put a stick under my covers (or anything else), please let me know. My backside will thank you.)

A Parent's Rights and Responsibilities

The other day, my nine-year-old called me the Worst Parent Ever because I made him sweep the floor. The exchange went something like this:

Him: I wish I had a different family.

Me: Why's that?

Him: Because I don't want to sweep the floor.

Me: Well, you'd have to do that in another family, so…

Him: No! No one else makes their kids do chores!

Me: [had to leave the room, because of the laughter bubbling up in my throat.]

Because my kids often operate under this idealistic view of others' lives and several have created elaborate fantasies about what it would be like to have different parents (mainly, they'd be able to play video games and watch YouTube videos all the time; they'd eat whatever they wanted—even if it was pizza every day; they'd never have to do chores; and they could stay up as late as they want.), I thought it might be helpful to compile a list of parenting rights and responsibilities that most parents—I can't definitively say all—use to run their families.

I've chosen, as I often do, letter form, to soften the blow.

Dear kids,

You have amazing contributions to make in the world, and your ideas are wonderfully creative. But the fact is, there are some rights and responsibilities that I cannot, in good conscience, sign over to you—not because you won't ever be capable of self-management, but because self-management takes time. It requires guidance from someone with more life experience and, thus, wisdom. I know you likely think you know more than your father and me, but we have lived a few more years and seen a few more things. That is just the nature of wisdom.

Right #1: The Hard Truth and Technology Time

I have the right to tell you when you're not acting like a decent human being and that when you're not acting like a decent human being, that means you have lost the privilege of exercising your technology time—no YouTube Minecraft videos, no video games, no movies.

I know, I know. Kids today practically live for technology; everyone has a phone! Their parents let them keep those phones in their rooms! They can use them anytime they want!

Sorry you got linked with parents who believe that creativity is stimulated by boredom. You will now be bored out of your mind. Just think of the wonders you'll create.

(And, no, you won't die.)

Right #2: Defining What it Means to Be a Decent Human Being

The revoking of your tech time privilege could be avoided if you acted like the person I know you are—a more-than-decent human being. You are a wonder. You are kind and capable.

Of course we all have funks and forget who we are, however momentarily, but decency is not an option. Speak in an honoring way. Look people in the eye. Acknowledge their presence and their words. Exchange ideas—even the angry, passionate, frustrated ones—in a calm-ish manner. Touch each other gently. Love in action, in thought, and in speech.

Why is this such a big deal? Because there is nothing more important than learning how to be decent, compassionate, empathetic humans, no matter how the other human beings throughout your day treat you, and you're not going to learn how to do it when your nose is stuck behind the screen of a computer or a phone or an iPad; you'll learn it interacting with others. Out in the world. In our cul-de-sac, in your classrooms, in our home. So if you're not acting like a decent human being to me—or your brothers—the virtual world is not what you need; the real world is.

So I have the right to deny you your virtual reality in lieu of your real reality.

You're welcome.

Right #3: Enforcing Bedtime

I have the right to change what time is bedtime, depending on how the day has gone. I understand that sometimes it confuses you that you and your brothers go to bed before the sun has even set, but I, as your mother, have the right to enforce this early bedtime. I enforce this early bedtime because all you've done for the last three hours is whine at me (this is a hypothetical example; there are many other reasons I might want to enforce an early bedtime), and I cannot take another whine-word. If I keep listening to this whine-talk, someone is going to break, and it's probably going to be me. And then you. So it's just better, all around, to move up bedtime. And if you don't like it, well. You can go to bed. Which you're already doing. So close your eyes, go to sleep, and let's all start over tomorrow.

Right #4: Eating What I Want—and Not Sharing

I have the right to eat chocolate or whatever dessert I desire, even if I haven't finished dinner. You do not. This is one of the painful things about being a kid. Adults get to do all sorts of things that kids aren't allowed—including eating chocolate for breakfast, for lunch, for dinner if we so desire—because we're fully grown. It doesn't hurt me to have chocolate before dinner, because I enjoy eating; it won't spoil my dinner. I'll eat all my vegetables in spite of this treat—because after vegetables is another chocolate reward. Sorry I can't share.

The same goes for restaurant take-out, kiwi (I can have as many as I like), and the cookies I just baked.

Right #5: Opting Not to Explain

I have the right to not explain the reasons for every action I take. I also have the right to change my answer to any question: for example, let's consider the questions, "May I have a cookie?" or "May I have a friend over?" or "May I please have tech time every day between the hours of 3 and 3:30?" Most days these answers would be yes, but some days my answer is a clear and definitive no.

I have the right to change my mind anytime I like, so if I

said yesterday that, yes, you could have a cookie today, but you're hitting your brother and calling him names repeatedly and you snap at me when I tell you to go put your school things away so they don't clutter up the living room, I have the right not to explain why I've now changed my mind: there is no treat today.

Which brings me to:

Right #6: The Changeable Mind

I have the right to change my mind without explanation. I know it bothers you—makes you die a little inside, maybe—not to know my reasons behind changing my mind, but the truth is, sometimes there aren't reasons; I don't want to have to admit that to you. And if it really bothers me that I don't have a good reason behind what I tell you to do or why I've said no to a request, then you can be assured that I'll think about it and probably will change my mind again tomorrow—in your favor. It will, however, not be in your favor if you badger, insist, insult, or ask the question incessantly.

It might behoove you to understand that sometimes there are things called Exceptions. An Exception is not a rule, as much as you would like to think that Saturday morning cartoons is a rule. Nope. We just had to clean for a birthday party, so we sat you down in front of the television for one Saturday out of the other fifty-one.

Right #7: Enforcing Consequences

I have the right to do what I said I would do—follow through with the consequences we agreed on before your offense.

This means that I can sit you on the bench for an entire afternoon, while I'm working near you in the kitchen, because this is the consequence for not staying in your bed during nap time like you were told, but, instead, climbing onto your dresser, reaching the fan, and dismantling it so it hangs from wires now. I have the right to deny you the pleasure of going over to a friend's house when you decide not to act like a friend to your brothers. I have the right to confiscate your bike if you use it irresponsibly, like riding through neighbors' yards, which you know is forbidden.

I have the right to take away your free time when it comes to things like making a mess of your room or scattering the laundry piles I just folded or spilling a whole bag of raw oats on the kitchen floor. You will clean your room, re-fold the laundry, and sweep up the oats, because all actions have consequences. We learn from our mistakes. And, also, I don't have the time or the energy to do it myself.

In exchange for these rights, parents also have certain responsibilities. You'll be glad to know this; we don't simply operate in a world of me, me, me. We owe you some things, too.

Responsibility #1: Safety

I have the responsibility to keep you from harming yourself or doing something stupid.

I know. You are boys, which means you daily face the temptation to walk—or run—up or down the stairs with your roller blades strapped to your feet like an extra appendage; you think sword fighting with shovels out in the backyard is worthwhile entertainment; you will fold yourselves into the rose bushes and believe it's an adequate hiding place.

As much as I possibly can, I have the responsibility, as your mother, to talk you out of such foolish actions, to entreat you to ponder—or at the very least, briefly consider—consequences before you execute your ideas, to show you better hiding places. In other words, my responsibility is keeping you alive.

It's a tall order for a mom of sons.

In a more practical sense, this responsibility explains why we don't let you ride your bike by yourself to school; it's not because we don't trust you to get there in one piece, it's because we can't trust the people who drive by you on their hurried way to work. This is also why the net around our trampoline must remain in place—no one wants you falling off in mid-jump and cracking a bone. Also, there's a twenty-foot drop beyond our fence, and your daddy and I don't want you getting any more brilliant ideas and attempting to bounce onto your daddy's shed, ricochet off, and fly into the wilderness.

Now I've just put an idea in your head, haven't I. Well, the net will catch you. For now.

This responsibility also means that sometimes I can't say yes to something you really, really want to do—like riding a skateboard down the stairs or jumping off the top bunk into the fan or trying to roll down a concrete hill face first.

Responsibility #2: Food

I have the responsibility to prevent you from eating until you throw up.

I know you're always hungry. And if someone were

watching us from the outside looking in, for a small moment in time—say, a single meal or a holiday get-together—they would think that I never feed you, because you go back for seconds and thirds and fourths, if no one's paying much attention. Sometimes you get really mad at me when I tell you that you can't have any more, you've already had enough—but the truth is, overeating is a really big deal. It's not good for your body, and, also, I don't fancy cleaning up your spaghetti puke, because that's not my idea of a fun Friday night. And it's happened before. And I learn from mistakes.

So I'm going to limit what you eat, and you can go ahead and sneak a pound of green grapes while I'm not looking, but don't come crying to me when you realize you've made a terrible mistake. You can't actually come crying to me; you're not getting off the toilet for the rest of the night.

I will do my best to reduce the kind of overeating that can make you sick, and I will daily brave your loud and fervent protests. At least it's only words coming out of your mouth.

You'll understand when you have your own kids.

Responsibility #3: Healing

I have the responsibility to kiss your hurts—no matter how dirty that toe is—and heal your sickness—even if I gag in the clean-up.

At some point you will stop coming to me with your physical wounds, because you'll realize my kisses don't actually have magic in them. But I will always be here to kiss and heal your hearts. I will rub your back when you're heaving into the toilet (just make it to the toilet, okay?). I will wrap my arms around you when you're drowning in anxiety or can't get out of bed because of the depression. I will kiss your heart when the first love breaks it. I will still be your healer.

Responsibility #4: Remembering

I have the responsibility to remember what it's like to be a kid.

Some parents don't remember what it's like to be a kid, but I don't ever want to forget. I want to remember, because I want to know that there is permission for me—and you—to play and be silly and have fun. I want to remember where you're coming from when you act like the whole world is splitting apart because you missed your technology time today and you still don't have much of a sense of time and don't comprehend that tomorrow you'll get a new chance; it's a brand new day, with a clean slate. I want to remember what it was like when your favorite toy went missing so I can deal with the aftermath.

I want to remember how scary the dark is (well, this I know well enough, I think) so I can ease you into sleep when you've lost the privilege of having a nightlight because you disassembled it during your nap time.

Remembering what it's like to be a kid means I get to empathize with every disappointing happenstance. And you get to feel understood.

Responsibility #5: Molding

I have the responsibility to mold you into an upstanding human being.

This means that there will be consequences for every choice you make. Some of them will be good; others will be undesirable.

You'll probably get tired of hearing me tell you that you need to think before you act, that you need to consider what you've done, that maybe you should apologize to your brother for being unkind. You will probably hate the words, "We need to have a talk," because this is the way we deal with conflict in our house; or "We are kind people," because one can never hear it too often; or "That is not an honoring way to speak. Please try again," because good communication is the most important part of relationships.

This responsibility also means we'll work on mundane things, like manners and chewing with your mouth closed and saying "excuse me" when a baritone burp erupts from your mouth. It means you'll be helping us repair all the holes you've made in the walls of our home, and you'll replace the things you break. It means that you'll pay for the library books you lose and the clothes you leave outside and the blinds you chew on and bend and tear apart.

You will get tired of a great many things—especially the consequences that accompany bad decisions. But I will never let up, because my responsibility is teaching you how to be human. I know who you are, and I will not watch you forget the wonder of you without fiercely stepping in.

It's not easy being a kid. It's not easy being a parent, either. You probably don't believe me about that, but one day you will. For now, I will keep my end of the bargain.

You'll thank us when you're grown.

Maybe.

(I hope you will. It's what I'm banking on, because we haven't started saving for retirement yet.)

A Mama's Hopes for Her Future Grown Children

Husband and I have the great privilege (and sometimes great annoyance) of being the go-to house on our block. All the neighborhood kids want to play here, because we have the best toys (hardly any, actually), and our backyard, thanks to Husband's love of mowing, is a natural wilderness, where ladybugs this spring have taken up residence in astonishing numbers. I guess they think we're lucky, too.

In this overgrowth of grass are likely a few snakes, some rodents, and maybe a black squirrel or two (something is responsible for chewing on every cucumber that ripens—and leaving half of it for us. I've been tempted to use the half that remains, but I haven't yet reached that stage of desperation.).

We also have a trampoline, which is the only thing that really matters when you're a boy brimming with repressed energy.

My theory is that the neighborhood kids like to spend so much time at our house because Husband and I are really cool parents. I mean, we typically stay out of the way and don't make eye contact (because when you make eye contact with kids, they think it's an invitation to ask for something), but, you know, they get to help dig that gigantic backyard hole on which our sons have been working for years, and that makes us cool.

Every morning during the school year, I walk my sons to their elementary school down the road—about five blocks. On the way, we pass middle school and high school students waiting for the bus. I hear their words and the subjects they discuss and note whether they move off the sidewalk for a woman with a baby in a stroller or whether they ignore completely that a mom with young children is trying to safely pass (many of them do ignore us, unfortunately, which either necessitates moving from the sidewalk to the street or pressing ourselves so close to a fence we may as well be in someone's backyard).

And then I have the distinct responsibility of fielding handfuls of snippy comments online, because I write for several different publications, and so all the people who like to personally attack writers make an appearance, too, some of them for shock value, some of them because they've never known another, better way to feel significant. They usually tell me one of two things I already know: (1) I'm failing as a parent and (2) I should lose some weight. Sometimes they punctuate their insults with other phrases like, "You're ugly," "You're disgusting," and "You're a whore." Thanks for the confidence boost, guys (and it is, unfortunately, mostly guys.).

Coming into contact with so many people is an honor, I believe, because it helps me to see who I want my kids to be like and who I don't. I hope that one day, when my kids are faced with whether to hurt someone's feelings or spew negativity or try on another identity—one that isn't quite as decent and kind—they will say, "My mama taught me better than that."

The way of our current world is to say exactly what you're thinking, because there aren't really any repercussions for it. We have the freedom of speech, after all. And it's not *always* bad to say what you're thinking. But it is *always* better to think before speaking, to run words through a filter: Is it kind? Is it necessary? Is it true—can it be proven? Will it hurt unnecessarily? These are the conditions I'd like my sons to consider before they open their mouths and speak what's on their mind.

I also hope that when my sons see a pregnant woman or an old, bent man standing in a waiting room while teenagers are sitting in the comfy seats, they will rise and say, "Please, sit," because their mama taught them better. Four years ago, I was in a doctor's office, eight months pregnant with twins (!!!), waiting for an appointment, and three young people were sitting in the padded rocking chairs playing on their phones while I stood and leaned against the wall, trying to get my feet to stop burning. They didn't even look up, didn't know I was there, didn't intuit how miserable I was standing in one place while two babies that already weighed more than ten pounds, collectively, were pressing on my sciatic nerve and making it hard to breathe. The quiet groaning I did was apparently not loud enough to demand their notice. It did, however, demand the notice of an old man, who gave up his seat willingly. I politely declined; he had to use a walker to stand up. By the time I was called back to the doctor my ankles were the size of a baby's head.

I hope my kids will say, "My mama taught me better than that" and quickly relinquish their seat.

When they're faced with a decision to be moral or to be underhanded, I hope they'll see the underhanded way and write, "My mama taught me better than that" all across it, in loopy or scratchy letters. When a kid hands them a drug, tells them they should try it, or when a girl offers them a risqué picture across the texting lines, or when their best friend asks if they'd like to street race up a country road, I hope they will say, "My mama taught me better than that." When a classmate makes fun of them for not getting an award, because he thinks an award tells us more about who we are than it actually does, I hope they say, "My mama taught me better than that."

I hope they'll give up their place or step aside out of the way for those who need space. I hope they'll speak kindly to all people, even those who aren't kind to them. I hope that before they write a response across the impersonal lines of the Internet, they will think through what they're saying and the way it could impact another human being, and I hope they'll contribute lovingly to the conversation without tearing people apart.

I hope they don't drive while glancing at their phones, and I hope they don't sit in front of the television and watch it all day, and I hope they don't try to hurt or sweep aside or bully people so they can get a leg up. I hope they know what it means to honor and cherish and be together and choose kindness and really, really love the people who come into their lives. I hope they understand that they are valued, and that they have a responsibility to value others.

I hope they will remember what I've taught them about injustice and doing what's right and the difference between people and their actions. I hope they never discount a person who does something wrong as if their wrong changes who they are. I hope they always fight for the broken-hearted and down-and-out.

When faced with a decision to choose what is easy over what is right, I hope they will always remember that their mama taught them better than that—and they will choose what's right.

THE SECRET LIFE OF MODERN PARENTING

All the Job Titles a Mom Wears

My sons occasionally find it necessary to ask who is the boss in our house. It's a strange question, since Husband and I divide pretty much everything equally; we are an egalitarian household. We generally respond that both of us are the boss, and they look confused, like they didn't think that two people could be co-bosses. I then explain to them that what I do and what their daddy does correspond one to another; we are on the same page in mostly everything (except conversations, because I mistakenly think, many times, that I've already told him something I actually haven't or vice versa.).

They know, by now, that Husband and I both wear lots of hats: Boss is only one of them. I'm a kids book author and write fiction stories for hours every weekday. But I'm also a nonfiction author, which means I'm an essayist, a poet, and a humorist. I edit and ghostwrite and freelance to help make ends meet.

I'm also a mother, which comes with its own subcategories of job titles and descriptions. Here are just a few of them:

1. Lunch Lady

Two days a week I pack all the lunches (Husband takes the other three days, according to our well-oiled schedule), because no matter how much I encourage my sons to do it on their own, they are so completely inefficient at guessing how much time they'll have at lunch that they will fill a whole container with almonds that take decades to chew, and they will return home with almost the same amount left—which they'll either leave in the sink so that water soaks them or they'll empty out in the trash, because second-day almonds aren't desirable. Both are annoyingly wasteful. (They do the same with Cereal Saturday. They'll pour an oversized bowl of cereal and eat only half of it. I'm still working on a solution for this—one that doesn't demand Husband and me getting out of bed before the sun comes up on our only day off.)

To complicate the autonomy dreams, my sons usually can't locate their lunch boxes, even though they've been "looking" for them for an hour. I guess you could add "Lunch Bag Finder" to the subcategory of this one, but who wants to get technical?

2. Light Fairy

I cannot tell you how many lights I have to turn off in our house. I have nagged my sons (and Husband) incessantly for many, many years about the importance of turning off the lights in a room that is unoccupied, but if I'm the only one home and I emerge from my bedroom, which is my home office, to get myself more water, there are ten billion lights blazing for all the world to see. We don't even have that many lights in our house. I will dutifully (but not uncomplainingly) turn them off, get myself a drink, and come back upstairs to see them blazing again. My sons aren't home. They must be right; we live with a ghost.

Any time we're leaving the house, I usher all my boys (including Husband) out of the house, and I check every room before leaving. My hand gets a cramp from turning off so many lights. When I slide into the passenger seat of our Honda Odyssey, to the annoyed (and ironic) refrain of "We're leaving late now," courtesy of the time keeper in our family, I will ask my sons how many lights they think were left on in the house. They always underestimate (zero), and then we get to have a fun conversation about energy conservation. They've heard it a billion times. Does it matter?

Clearly not. The next time we leave, there will, if possible, be even more lights left on.

3. Nose Wiper

It doesn't matter if Husband is around, my little ones will come to me with the smallest sheet of toilet paper, clueless to the fact that there's enough snot on their nose and cheeks to eat this tiny piece of paper within a second of application. I have a queasy stomach sometimes, which means I'm not all that stable around things coming out the openings of my kids' bodies—except for diapers, of course; I could change diapers all day, and I do. I can handle diaper mess, but vomit and snot are two other things entirely. Faced with the tiny square and the massive mess on a snotty face, I'll send my son back into the bathroom for a larger piece of toilet paper. He'll come back with two squares instead of half of one.

Sometimes they'll even come to me without a tissue or anything I could use to wipe their noses. They just want a hug, and I will have the grand privilege of wearing snot on my shoulder for the rest of the day. It's a great accessory and goes with everything. Nothing shouts "mother" like Snot Shoulder.

4. Hurt Kisser

This job doesn't last long enough, in my opinion; they age out of it quickly. I miss it—at least until one of my sons wanders in with a hurt on the bottom of his foot that doesn't have a shoe but does have a large cake of dirt—or is that dog poop?—on the underside. And then I have to grit my teeth and kiss the underside of that foot, because my kisses are magical, and one day they won't be.

Things I have kissed to kiss away hurts: a snotty nose (I don't like snot as much as my kids do), a stinky toe, a finger that I saw up the kid's nose a few minutes ago. You have to have a steely stomach to be a mom. And we've already established I don't have that. I've trained my gag reflex to resolve itself invisibly. I've had many, many moments to practice.

5. Manners Teacher.

This particular job is something my kids would call one of the annoying parts of my personality. They would also say that a more accurate title would be Manners Nagger, not Manners Teacher. But that's only a technicality; they think it's nagging because I have to remind them so many times to stop smacking; I don't like to see food being chewed. I tell them often not to talk while someone else is talking; to clean up after themselves; to use their please and thank you; to say, at the very least, "Excuse me" when an earth-quaking burp disrupts the table; to wait until everyone is finished before they ask for seconds.

They think these reminders are lame. They don't know they'll thank me later, when they're interested in finding a life partner and they discover other people aren't all that attracted to heathen habits like showing what kind of food they're eating or rudely interrupting conversations or burping (or worse) at all junctures and in all silences. Boys who spray it instead of saying it need to learn some manners.

6. Animal Tamer

My sons often remind me of wild animals. They are constantly on the prowl, and I am usually constantly on the move, trying to keep them out of all the things they could possibly use to entertain themselves. I don't keep them out of everything; I save my energy for the dangerous things. And the more annoying things. I remind them that people don't tear up things with their teeth, that people don't generally jump on couches, that people don't willingly destroy everything in their path. And they remind me that I'm living with a collection of wild and rowdy boys, and sometimes it's okay to let things go.

There are, of course, more jobs. My résumé gets longer every day. And with all these hats and jobs, sometimes I get confused and overstep my bounds and become the Sentimental Mother when I should be the Invisible Mother and I accidentally tell my son I love him in front of all his ten-year-old friends.

Will he thank me for that later?

Likely not.

The Pressures that Sit on Modern Parents' Shoulders

We're hurtling toward the end of the school year and all the madness it contains. There are field trips and three field days and teacher appreciation activities and all kinds of end-of-the-year programs that parents are invited (expected?) to attend.

As I drag my heels into this brief breathless season that comes back around every year, I find myself thinking that there is so much more expected of parents today than there used to be.

I had one end-of-year program in elementary school—when I graduated the fifth grade. My sons? They have a reading awards ceremony, a dance off, a moving-up-to-the-next-grade celebration, an end-of-the-school-year party, a P.E. Day (I might be making up that last one, but who would even know?). And they're all on different days of the week. For each kid. I have three in school right now. I should just camp out at the school.

For the holidays, my teacher got a hand-written note from me, along with maybe a small chocolate bar or the cliché apple. Now you walk into a teacher's classroom before the holiday break in December and her entire desk is filled with homemade gifts and large party baskets and gift cards for $100 to the local restaurant she marked as her favorite when she filled out the teacher information sheet at the beginning of the year (which I lost four days later). For weeks, I've been getting notices about "Treat the staff" and "Teacher Appreciation Week" (with suggested gifts for each day of the week) and "it's-the-teacher's-birthday-so-let's-pool-money-to-buy-her-a-crazy-cool-gift" and then, when all that's said and done, there's the end-of-the-schoolyear gift.

To reiterate, I have three children in separate classes at school. They are all in the gifted program with another teacher. They have an art teacher, a music teacher, and a P.E. teacher. That's seven teachers. Buying gifts for all of them is a second job.

Now. I'm not saying that teachers don't deserve to be pampered; please hear me in that. Teachers are saints. Being stuck in a room with twenty five-year-olds? That sounds like torture to me, but there are teachers who live for it. I can't help but admire them. And, also, be very, very glad for them because I tried homeschooling once and threatened my ornery five-year-old with calling the cops because he wouldn't sit down and copy the handwriting passage that my lesson plans said he had to do (who said living a strong-willed life with other strong-willed people was easy?). That was my wakeup call. I was not made to be a teacher.

So I appreciate them immensely.

It's just that when we add all this extra stuff on top of the daily challenge of parenting, it feels practically impossible to do either one well. Kids are complaining that they're the only ones in school who didn't bring their teacher a gift today, and one teacher is asking where the seven-year-old's permission slip went (I'm not really sure. I think someone might have run out of toilet paper yesterday, and a brother was being creative and resourceful? I don't think you want that one back.) and another is asking if I got that flier they sent home about the math night they're having at school, because of course my nine-year-old expressed interest in attending.

Sometimes I wish we could step back in time, to what seemed like simpler days (although the grass is always lusher on the clueless side, isn't it?). I'm all for sending a teacher a nice note to let her know just how much I appreciate what she's done in my kid's life, but when I think about preparing seven teacher gifts for the five days (that's thirty-five total gifts) of Teacher Appreciation Week—the money it might demand or the time it would take to make my own—I feel a bit overwhelmed. I mean, I'm not even keeping up with all the papers, a fact proven by the five-inch-thick stack on the counter. And I just wrote in the seven-year-old's reading folder, which hasn't been signed since November, "He's reading. I promise," and called it a day.

How am I supposed to keep my head above water?

Every time I turn around, someone is asking me if I want to volunteer for something. Someone is inviting me to an after-school event. Someone is telling me about another award ceremony that's scheduled—an award ceremony for passing the STAAR test, an award ceremony for reading a certain number of books, an award ceremony for passing the fourth grade and the second grade and first grade, an award ceremony for making this cool thing in art class, even though you can't really tell what it's supposed to be.

I'm glad my sons are awesome. But I don't need more award ceremonies.

Have we always been this busy? My sons have no extracurricular activities, because they're all still in elementary school and we've purposefully kept them out of organized sports and other time-consuming activities. What happens when they move up to middle school? Do we get exponentially more overwhelmed? Is this a proper way to live?

Today's parenting world comes with so many pressures. It's not easy to keep up. But as long as teachers are willing to accept "those parents" who can't keep up with anything, then I'll keep trucking away, because, like I said, I threatened my oldest with jail time back when he was five and we experimented with homeschooling. That's not the sort of mom I'd like to be. I'd rather be drowning in papers and events and ceremonies and looking, endlessly, for a pen with which to sign too many agendas.

So, at the end of the school year, I plaster on my biggest smile, square my shoulders, and take my failing "School Parent" grade with grace and humor, because there's always next year—

To fail again.

The Mysterious Lure of Screens: a Love/Hate Story

I am always staggered by the obsessive magnetism screens have on my sons.

I've never been a screen person; when my siblings would sit and watch hours of after-school television, I would read in the living room, to have company. I could tune out every voice on the show—so well that when my mom came home and called my name, I wouldn't hear her. Books captivated me the same way screens captivate my children.

Part of it could be that I don't really understand technology. Put me in front of a computer that does all sorts of amazing things, and I will likely only be able to figure out one of those amazing things, if I'm lucky. And someone shows me. Any time I have a problem with my computer—if my screen locks up or something of the sort—I will immediately call Husband (thankfully we both work from home). I don't have the patience or the time to try to solve the problem myself.

Husband is convinced that I could figure things out if I applied myself—by studying technology, becoming more familiar with it, trying things for myself. I tell him my brain can only hold so many things, and technology is a very low priority for me. He tells me technology is necessary for the future. I tell him I have very little brain remaining after passing on my brilliance to six gifted sons.

Six gifted sons who, when technology comes out of hiding, transform into insects drawn to light.

Husband could be upstairs working in our bedroom, and the whispers of a video might traipse down the stairs, unintentionally (he gets distracted from time to time), and my sons' backs will straighten and their heads will cock. I can't even hear it, and I had my ears tested six years ago when I suffered bouts of vertigo, and the doctor said my ears are so good I could hear a rabbit crossing the street outside my house. Before I know what's happening, my sons are clomping up the stairs, racing one another to see who can locate the playing video first. Judging by the crash and the immediate crying, they're all in a pile outside my bedroom, which is where Husband works. By the time they untangle themselves, the video will be done.

It matters not.

Husband will use his phone while cooking dinner and one simple note will play a preamble to a commercial, and my sons will barge in from the backyard to see what's playing. He will accidentally turn something on while he's holed away in the bathroom, and they will be up the road at their friend's house, but they will come slamming through the door to discover what he's watching, which is surely better than the basketball game they were playing in the street. He will reach for something in his pocket, which is where he typically keeps his phone, and they are already swarming him.

It's like a seventh sense.

I can't show Husband a picture of something without a kid hanging off my arm, begging to see it, too. He can't mention a video he sent me (which I rarely watch) without someone saying, "Can we watch it, too?" We can't leave a phone unattended without someone picking it up and finger painting it with the juice from the apple they're eating as they try to figure out our passcode (I'm talking about you, twins).

My older sons are permitted a bit of technology time every day, once homework and reading time and tidying-their-room time and everything else they're expected to do is finished. It's like surgically removing a tooth to pry those devices out of their hands once their allotted time is up. They will clutch their device like it's the answer to life, and once the devices are hidden again, they'll talk for forty hours straight about what they did during their trip to Technology Land today. They'll talk so long my eyes start to glaze over and I feel like I'll pass out, because my body knows when I need to escape from a dangerous situation, and, rather than run and be caught, it sometimes likes to play dead.

I can try to talk to them while they have the devices in front of their faces, but they will not hear a word I say.

Recently we introduced reading ebooks on the iPad. I did this for a number of reasons. I have, in the past, been very hesitant to do it. But I'm an author. Which means that part of my sales are ebooks for kids. So I wanted to see if my sons would actually enjoy reading on a device.

That was only one reason, though. Another is that I'm

tired of paying library fines for the books we can't find in our house. It's like we live in the middle of a black hole, and it swallows socks, shoes, and library books on an annoyingly regular basis. We have places for all of these things. They don't get there.

I thought ebooks might help with this problem. I'm still partial to the hard copies of books, but ebooks allow me to check out a large number of reading materials for my sons—and automatically return them.

Surprisingly, my sons didn't enjoy reading on a device. They like to feel the pages, same as me. The ebooks held no allure for them.

This got my hopes up for an eventual loss of love for all devices, but, of course, my hopes were much too high. They still drop everything when they hear their daddy whispering to me, "Hey, did you see this video? You should watch it real quick" and barrel into my lap and head-butt each other (not on purpose; it's just the nature of finding the best angle from which to see) until there are so many heads now I can't see anymore.

I know that one day my sons will likely be doing school work on their devices. I won't be able to limit their interaction with technology forever. But I do what I can, for now, and hope that one day they'll understand.

If they don't, I'll just bill them for all the library books I had to replace and we'll call it even.

Kids and Allergies: a Short Examination

Parents today live in a world where kids are kept close to home and parents call out other parents for their seeming parental deficiencies and folders must be signed every single day or a school will call home.

And, also, allergies abound.

It's become a measure of status to be a kid with an allergy. At least according to my kids and their friends.

I'm not trying to make light of a very real danger. I realize that there are kids with severe allergies who could die if they sniff peanut butter or eggs or shellfish. I realize this is serious.

It's just that the other day, my seven-year-old came home and said, "Mama, I found out I'm allergic to tomatoes today."

"Oh, yeah?" I said, knowing better. This kid isn't allergic to any food. None of my kids are. I'm super fortunate to have escaped the misery of food allergies. "How do you know?"

"Well, this girl was sitting next to me eating tomatoes, and I sneezed," my son said. His blue eyes fixed on me expectantly. I looked back at him expectantly, thinking surely this wasn't the end of the story. Lip swelling? Upset stomach? Skin rash, maybe?

Wait. Only a sneeze?

"Maybe you just needed to sneeze," I said.

"No," he said. "I'm allergic." And then he skipped off to tell all his neighborhood friends that he was allergic to tomatoes, blissfully unaware that we'd had tomatoes in our chicken salad last night and he hadn't died. Or sneezed.

This is the same kid who once told our pediatrician that he had a milk allergy. The pediatrician raised her eyebrows in my direction, and I shook my head, and she smiled a little knowing smile, as if all the kids were saying things like that these days. And maybe they are. Maybe it really has become the desirable thing, from a kid's point of view, to be a kid with allergies. The allergy kids get to sit at their own table. They get to have special lunches and snacks. They're given different treats at the holiday parties.

The allergy kids get a little more attention from their teacher, who has to watch what they're eating and what they're touching and whether they need the nurse's help managing an allergic reaction. Every kid wants more attention. Attention is love. I get it.

All that can seem like a luxury to kids on the other side.

Kids who don't have food allergies think having an allergy is some kind of "I'm more important" badge, because, at the depths of their hearts, they're all just looking to be distinct and unique and set apart. Or, at the very least, noticed.

Kids with allergies also get to avoid undesirable foods—which, for my seven-year-old, includes most vegetables.

As a much more logical adult, I know there's nothing cool about having an allergy. I know it's dangerous and inconvenient and super scary.

My seven-year-old has several classmates with food allergies. I don't envy their parents at all. I wish allergies didn't exist so we didn't have to worry about the well being of children when it comes to food. I can't imagine how worrisome it is, sending a kid to school with a majority of other kids who don't have allergies and don't think about the danger that can exist in a simple sandwich.

I also wish, more selfishly, that food allergies didn't exist so my second grader wouldn't come home every other day to tell me that he's allergic to something else because his leg went numb after he ate it (pretty sure this is because of the way he sits on his legs at the cafeteria table; I've eaten lunch with him before, so I've seen it myself, the way he folds himself into a contortionist's proportions) or because his nose got itchy or because he lost a hair on the back of his head.

Until kids start understanding the gravity of food allergies —that they are something that can kill a person and that they're taken very, very seriously—I imagine we might see more of this "I Have Allergies" phenomenon. I've seen it in more than just my second grader. When a neighborhood kid comes over, he's always got an allergy (even though I check with parents). One kid is pretty insistent that he doesn't eat carrots or celery or broccoli or cucumbers or beets or cauliflower, because he's allergic to them (guess he'll go hungry at our house). Right now, to all these kids who don't have them, allergies can seem like a distinctive privilege—just like having glasses can seem like a distinctive privilege until you're the kid who can't see two feet in front of your face and your parents slap on you some ugly purple frames that reach more than halfway down your cheeks and you have to wear them every day because you just realized the world is full of color instead of blurry fog and you end up wearing them for three years instead of the suggested one year even though you have to superglue their earpieces back on (thanks, Mom. I haven't forgotten.).

So I've tried explaining to my son that having an allergy is no small thing, that it's actually a really big deal, that we can't just play around with those words, "I have an allergy," because there are people who could die if they eat what they're allergic to, but all he said was, "Well, my legs hurt when I eat salad. Maybe I'm allergic to lettuce."

Well. He's still young. I'll wait until he's old enough to spell "asphyxiation" before I try again.

Which means we might be waiting forever, because spell check just helped me out.

Dance Party Ethic According to Kids

Dance night has reached epic proportions in our house. We schedule a dance night about once a week, because sometimes you just need music and moves to leach all the frustration and pain from your limbs. It's hard living as a family, and the times that we've cut loose, we can feel everything between us leaking out of our insides (including but not limited to smelly farts). We'll usually end the night in a pile of giggles.

Here are some lessons I've gleaned from my children pertaining to dance party ethic:

Principle 1: Just do whatever comes naturally.

If you want to throw in a few hip thrusts, that's perfectly understandable. If you want to do a cross between jumping jacks and pliés, have at it. However. If you want to grab your crotch area, which seems pretty typical of all my boys and which they have NEVER seen their daddy nor their mother do, ever, this is not your unlimited opportunity to have a ball (no pun intended). Modesty is important, too. I have an unfortunate (and yet extremely affectionate) memory of the oldest dancing during a preschool Thanksgiving program. He brazenly introduced this move to people who do not live in our house. He was three, and I don't know where he picked up the move; I think it might just come standard in males. His daddy and I, of course, talked to him about modesty—but he was three.

We talk much more about modesty now. I think my sons are finally starting to get it.

On another note, if you want to clear the dance floor with your interpretation of break dancing, feel free. If you want to walk around on stiff legs and pretend *that's* a dance, do it. If you want to simply bob your head and raise your eyebrows, that's dancing, too.

There are no standards for good or bad dancing in this house (except, of course, the modesty piece).

Principle 2: Say, "Watch this!" every other minute.

This suggestion comes with a clarifying addendum: if the person you're trying to impress—like, say, your mom—is ignoring you completely because they're really into their own interpretive dance, set yourself up right beside them so they either trip on you and break their kneecap or they catch themselves at the last minute and strain an important muscle in their back that will protest every time they take a step. That way they'll calm down enough to give you their undivided attention.

Mission accomplished. Well done, little dancer.

Principle 3: Try to breakdance and unfortunately get hurt.

You didn't know the carpet was so hard, did you? Those break dancers you've seen on YouTube videos make it look so easy, but this is actually a skill that you can't do unless you're made of rubber or you've been practicing for years. Although my seven-year-old almost has it down. He can spin for ages on his head. Who knew it was so big (I did, when he was born).

Breakdancing should be reserved for parents—who will likely not take you up on the challenge, because things hurt more when you're older. I'm convinced the only way to properly breakdance is to be younger than thirty. After thirty, your limbs don't work the same anymore—and neither does your pain response. I didn't always complain for days about a rug burn. Aging is hard.

Principle 4: Make sure there's a cartwheel somewhere in your performance so someone gets kicked in the face.

This happens every single time. Every single time. Someone's feeling a little clever and adventurous, and they misjudge the space they have in which to execute an efficient cartwheel. We don't have a large living room, and there are eight of us.

This probably goes without saying, but if you're a parent, cartwheels aren't recommended. You will either kick yourself in the face, accidentally (if you're still that limber) or, if you're like Husband, you'll rip your best and favorite pants. Better to stick with your feet on the floor so your kids won't laugh at you forever and say, "Remember that time?" even when in the presence of company.

Principle 5: Lose some part of your clothing.

My sons cannot make it through an entire song without stripping some piece of clothing off their little bodies. Most of the time it's, predictably, their pants. They're too constrictive, they say. Close the windows, then, I say. No one's looking, they say. And I realize I probably should have closed the windows in the first place; if someone happens by our house during the middle of a dance party, they might think the same bolt of lightning is striking us all, at the same time.

Honestly, by the time the dance party is over, I want to strip some of my clothing, too, because it's hard work dancing like there's no tomorrow. Like no one is watching. Like I have not a care in the world. I might have been able to handle a hammer fest like this when I was younger, but, like I said: aging. It's hard.

My most often-repeated phrase at the close of Family Dance Night is: "Where are your pants?" Which is followed, almost in the same breath, by their answer: "I don't know."

Principle 6: Make sure you're moving all your body parts.

My sons are some of the most fluid and expressive dancers I've ever had the privilege of observing. They're so very creative when they're dancing, and kids are like Gumby. They bend in astonishing, seemingly unnatural ways. When they are dancing, they move every single body part—if it's not moving, well, they'll use their hands to move it.

Watch out, Whip it Nae Nae. They are completely uncivilized.

Principle 7: Don't worry about the beat. You can make up your own.

My twins are probably the worst dancers in the house.

They usually just jump around—off the beat, because they have a little trouble listening and possibly processing what they hear (testing is pending). This trouble finding the beat—listening for it—also reaches into the way they listen to instructions: they're typically two or three beats behind. For example: they stall on the word "treat" in the sentence, "I'll give you a treat once you put your school stuff away and unpack your lunch supplies."

Oh well. We're safe within the privacy of our living room, so it's not like anyone will see them. Unless Husband is filming, in which case I'm going to sit this one out, lest my moves overshadow theirs. No sense in being the star of the show; I'll let my sons have that role.

Principle 8: Laugh at your parents' attempts to dance.

Laugh so hard you almost pee your pants. They look so silly, don't they? This is called The Hammer, kid, and it's the greatest dance there ever was. Want to know what The Electric Slide looks like? How about the Jiggy?

My sons laugh every time we try to show them what real dance moves are—The Tootsie Roll, the Carlton, and Husband's favorite, the Butterfly. I guess not all kids can appreciate the genius of the '90s.

They do know the Jump, though, made popular by Kris Kross, even though kids today will argue with you until they're red in the face because they think they made up that move. I know from personal experience.

Principle 9: Smell like a wet dog by the time it's all over.

My sons are so sweaty by the time our Family Dance Party

is over that the house just took a giant step toward Locker Room, instead of Home. And that's nothing compared to how I smell.

So my sons make fun of Husband and me and call our antiquated moves "dorky." Well, I saw one of them attempting The Butterfly when he thought I wasn't looking.

I guess we're not so bad after all.

However. I will not be taking my modern dance expertise public anytime soon. The privacy of my own home is a good enough place to unleash these wicked awesome moves.

Phrases I've Come to Expect From Summer

Summer is in full swing at the Toalson home. Summer means a lot of things to parents, but what it mostly means to me is that my word count—listened-to words, that is, not written ones; I can't seem to write when all the kids are home—increases from four billion to six hundred forty billion. Daily.

When they're not fighting or bouncing off walls, my sons are talking. They're telling me every detail of their forty-minute dreams (my dreams aren't that long, but okay), what they plan to build out of the LEGO pieces today, and how they managed to live when they tried to do a double somersault off the trampoline onto the treehouse fort (I'd rather not hear about that one, thanks.).

In all this talking, there are some phrases that have become tired refrains in our house—and I'm not talking about the dreams or the plans or the daring feats. I'm talking about my name, "Mama," connected with pretty much anything and, more specifically, the following:

"I'm hungry."

This one made it to the top of the list because it's the most frequently repeated phrase in my home. It doesn't matter if my sons ate a hearty breakfast of a dozen scrambled eggs five minutes ago. They're still hungry. If they eat four sandwiches and five pounds of carrots for lunch, two minutes later they'll be hungry. If we fill their bellies with a steaming six bowls of chicken noodle soup, they will be hungry in less than ten minutes.

We're not a snacking family. My sons have to wait until 3 in the afternoon to get a snack, and if you were to ask them, this would be the most horrible torture of all. We're the meanest parents ever. They're starving, all because of us and our silly rules.

"I'm bored."

There are so many things to do in my house. We have a really cool house. We have a home library with thousands of books they could read. They all have scooters and bikes and a safe cul-de-sac in which to ride them. We have a trampoline, a treehouse fort, a swing set, a relatively big backyard. We have an art cabinet stocked with art supplies. We have writing journals waiting to be filled. There is no limit to activity and creative possibility in this home.

So my typical response to the "bored" phrase is, "All of life is a playground for the curious," followed closely by, "How about you do the laundry and I'll be bored. Deal?"

This never accomplishes what I'd like it to accomplish.

"Can we watch a movie?"

For some reason, my sons think summertime is synonymous with watch-all-the-movies-you-can time. They like to remind their father and me that they don't have school tomorrow, so they should be able to watch something. Husband and I aren't really screen people. We like our kids to be bored. The best ideas (and also the most disastrous, but that's neither here nor there) arise from boredom. We want our sons to use their creative brains to make something beautiful. And preferably not messy. But we try not to be picky.

They will sulk and complain when we answer this question in the negative. They'll tell us that all their friends get to watch as many movies as they want over the summer, to which I typically reply exactly what my mother used to: "Well, if all your friends jumped off a cliff, would you do it, too?"

They love this about as much as I loved it as a kid.

"It's too hot out there."

My sons have mandatory outdoor playing time between 4:30 and 5:30 p.m., which coincides with cooking-dinner time. Purposefully. I can't have monkeys swinging from the rafters while I'm trying to brown some turkey meat for tonight's broccoli extravaganza that they'll all complain about if they could see what I'm cooking. This way they get to be surprised and I get to have a little peace.

The problem is that here in South Texas, the summer temperature hits two thousand degrees on a good afternoon (you don't want to know what the bad afternoons look and feel like). I solve this problem by setting out a pitcher of ice water and an assortment of cups they'll fight over until they knock the pitcher off the table and lose all the ice water and commence lapping it up from the worn boards of the deck, because it's fun to act like animals.

"My brother hit me."

Every other minute my sons are fighting and tattling. The tattling usually comes from the five-year-old twins, because my older sons are good at working out their disagreements. By socking each other in the mouth. And laughing about it.

"You're the worst mom ever."

I hear this every time I tell them they can't have a snack; all of life is a playground for the curious; if all their friends were jumping off a cliff, would they; and they have to play outside. I also hear it when I tell them that they can't wear their swim trunks for the twelfth day in a row; no, we're not going to the pool today; and treats aren't assured them every day.

That's okay. I know they still love me, and sooner or later (probably later), they'll realize I'm not actually the worst mom ever.

"How much longer until school starts?"

Okay, that one's me.

But I suspect that toward the end of the summer they'll be asking this one, too. Family togetherness is great, but it's also nice to have time away from each other, to ease into your old routines, to have something to do with the endless hours of your day. And then, a week after school starts, they'll be wishing it was over.

Honestly, I'm glad we have summertime together. It's a special time of bonding over boredom (although I haven't been bored since I was eight) and snuggling for a few seconds before they're off and running and playing together. This year I have five of them going off to school, and I'm sure the quiet house will be fantastic for the first couple of days, and then it will feel unnaturally eerie. I'll miss them, like I always do.

Well, at least I'll have some food to eat for once.

8 Steps that Comprise a Strong-Willed Child's Meltdown

The other day I went to pick up my younger sons from the elementary school right down the road, because the oldest, who normally walks his brothers home, had stayed for LEGO League practice. As soon as I returned home, however, Husband bounded down the stairs to tell me that my oldest son wanted to come home, too.

"He can walk home," I said.

"He wants you to come get him," Husband said.

I was mildly annoyed, because we live four blocks from the school, and I didn't want to pack up his five brothers and take another trip there and back.

Husband gave me a Look. And by that Look, I knew it would be a rough afternoon. Something had happened. Something to upset our strong-willed, highly emotional child.

I walked into the school office the second time around. My scowling boy was waiting on a bench. I didn't say anything. I wanted to wait until we were alone before I questioned him. When we were, I said, "Why'd you decide to come home?"

"I didn't feel like staying," he said. "It takes me a while to get back into school." They'd just returned from the holiday break. He waited a minute, and then he said, "When I get home, can I have tech time?"

I knew this was the real, hidden reason he wanted to come home: if he'd stayed for LEGO League, he might not have had enough time remaining between getting home and eating dinner to have his precious technology time.

There was a big problem: He had lost the privilege of tech time the day before because he had mouthed off to Husband and me, during a show of anger.

To reiterate, this son is our strong-willed, sticky-brained, highly emotional child (he is only one of several, but he inducted us into the Beaten Down Parent Club early and efficiently). When he was two, we called him our little lawyer. When we told him it was bedtime, he would say, "Well, I think I'm going to stay up for five more minutes because…" and lay out a long defense of reasons. Impressively creative, but also irritating. He argued—argues still—about pretty much everything.

Some deliberations with this child last a few minutes, some a little longer (as in hours). In case you've never experienced the magnificence that is a strong-willed child's meltdown, here's an exhaustive breakdown.

Step 1: Immediate crumbling, which manifests in crying hysterically (5-7 minutes)

It's the end of the world, and he is going to prove it.

Step 2: Pleading for another chance (5-7 minutes)

This step comes with a lot of crying and bargaining: I'll follow every rule you have, I'll do anything to make it up, I'll babysit my brothers (as if), I'll try to do better, I'm sorry, please give me one more chance, this is how you can prove you love me, I didn't mean to, I made a mistake, please give me one more chance, please give me one more chance, pleasepleaseplease give me one more chance.

Step 3: Insulting (2-3 minutes)

Phrases during this stage include (but are not limited to; strong-willed children are usually also quite creative): You're the worst mom ever, I wish you were dead, I wish I had parents who loved me more, I wish I could have a more loving mom, I wish I lived with someone else, you just hate me, you hate tech time, you hate pleasure, you want to make my life miserable, you are my worst enemy.

He thinks this will help his case.

Step 4: Pleading again (10-15 minutes)

He repeats Step 2 to see if it will work this time, especially after he's efficiently insulted his parent.

Step 5: Diplomatic conversation (20-30 minutes)

Here's his guiding principle for this step: Lay out all the reasons you should be able to have technology time. Say your teacher needs you to do something on the computer, it makes you a better reader and writer, it develops your imagination, it actually will make you fall behind in school if you don't get to have technology time today, you might not get a job when you're older because you didn't get to have technology time today, your creative brain is going to wither away because you didn't get to have technology time today.

Expert Tip: Make sure you use all the things your parents have said are important to them.

Step 6: Pleading (5 minutes)

Repeat Steps 2 and 4.

Step 7: Grieving elsewhere (1 minute)

Before he leaves, he will make sure to say, "Fine," ball his fists, and stomp to his room, where he will cry very, very, loudly. It's required that the volume is loud enough to hear anywhere in the house. It may not result in sympathy points, but, at the very least, it's alarming.

Step 8: Singing

Meh. He's over it. He'll start singing his favorite song and happily building amazing fortresses (that he might not have built if buried in technology time? It's not the proper time to ask; we'll get to that later) with his LEGO blocks.

This strong will is difficult to handle right now. I know it will serve him well later, which is why I engage it rather than ignore or crush it. Engaging with a strong-willed child, rather than dogmatically shutting them down at every turn, teaches them how to effectively communicate; you can revisit your conversation later to help them understand better techniques that might benefit them in the future. We can all use some training in respectful deliberations—and what better way to learn than to teach a child? Engaging and yet still holding your position (as in, not giving in to technology time, no matter how much he wants it) teaches strong-willed children resilience in the face of a setback.

Engagement helps when you yourself have an iron will.

See, Mom? There's a reason I was so stubborn—to better raise my own strong-willed children.

Also: I'm sorry.

Noises that Strike Fear in the Hearts of Parents

What is it about quiet that males don't understand?

In my house of six boys and one man, I am sorely outnumbered in the gender department, which means I am, on a typical day, run over not just physically, by boys flinging their bodies every which direction (I always get caught in their crossfire, because I'm not that fast on my feet anymore), but also vocally. I am the quietest voice in my house. When I yell (which isn't often, I feel I should admit), I sound about the same as my sons' normal volume for talking, telling stories, and tattling. My yell cannot even come close to their decibel volume when whining, complaining, or asking a question for the four billionth time.

As you might imagine, I hear thousands of words every day. I also hear many, many other sounds throughout the course of my day with sons. Some of these sounds strike fear in my heart (though nothing close to the kind of fear I feel when the house is completely silent and all my children are home).

Here are a few of those fearful sounds.

1. LEGO pieces clacking against each other.

This sound doesn't always bring fear; sometimes it brings relief, because it means my sons have found something to do besides flip off couches and turn down beds and fight over Pokémon cards. However, when I hear the sound that is so specifically LEGOs and I have not given permission for those LEGOs to come out, fear fuels my feet and overthrows my brain so I will run into an explosion of pieces with no shoes protecting my tender heels from Ninjago swords and Spider-Man webs.

Unauthorized LEGO play hardly ever resembles anything but a colorful explosion arranging itself into a walking minefield. There are a variety of reasons for this: Kids are in a hurry, trying to get into something they have not yet been permitted to get into; kids aren't as efficient at untying the strings around the LEGO carpet; and, simply, kids. Explosions come with the territory. I learned that the first time I changed my oldest son's diaper and realized I hadn't waited long enough.

2. Bangs and thumps in the bathroom.

Of course I don't watch my sons in the bathroom; this lack of privacy is only reserved for two particular sons who love to play with plungers, still, even though they're four. We thought they'd grow out of this bliss, but I can confidently report that they have not. They have also not grown out of opening all the Band-Aids and attaching them to the floor, dipping entire toilet paper rolls in the toilet just to see what will happen, and explaining their deviance with nonsensical words like, "I did it because my poo was really bad."

Uhhh....what?

It probably shouldn't be surprising. These two, when they

were babies, regularly waited until nap time to empty their bowels, remove their diapers, and delightedly smear their feces all over their cribs, their sheets, their walls, and themselves. For forty days. We turned onesie pajamas backward, cut holes, tied them with zip ties, Duct taped—and they still found a way to practice their smelly art.

3. The words, "Let's play The Hitting Game."

My sons come up with some really interesting means of entertainment. The Hitting Game is one of them. They play it out on the trampoline, and it's supposed to be fun. The problem is that it always ends one way: a bleeding something and a kid wailing.

Yesterday it was a bleeding toe, the day before that an ankle. This is likely because our sons have toe-talons, rather than nails, because they don't understand (or care) about hygienic practices like trimming nails.

4. The gurgling sound of vomit.

In my house, there's almost always a lead-up. Words ("I feel sick"), a cough, the patter of feet trying to make it to the bathroom. I appreciate that last one. Not so much the one who comes to me and says, "I feel sick," and before he gets the sentence out, I'm wearing the kind of perfume a shower won't even wash off.

5. The words, "I need to go potty."

These words are particularly annoying in the following cases: (1) when we're on a long trip and I told them to make sure they used the potty before we left and we just pulled out of our driveway, (2) when we're stuck in traffic on a highway in the middle of nowhere, (3) when I'm in a store with a basket full of groceries, and (4) when we're traveling and we stopped three minutes ago.

My sons are notorious for thinking they don't have to go to the bathroom on a regularly scheduled bathroom break and then realizing, five minutes later, that they actually have to go. Really badly.

6. Pounding feet at 6 a.m. on a Saturday.

This is especially true when I forgot to hide all the technology devices in my bedroom.

7. Silence.

Silence means something fishy in the life of a child. It means someone's doing something he's not supposed to be doing, someone's making a grand mess (for the little ones in my house, this means they've located a permanent marker and are having a ball), or someone's hiding.

I prefer the latter, but I rarely let silence reign without investigating the cause.

Sometimes I'm pleasantly surprised—all the kids are reading.

8. Excessive laughter

This is about as scary as silence and usually means the same thing.

9. The words, "I'm telling."

In the summertime, I hear these words so many times I lose count. Tattlers aren't the least bit of fun. Also, I don't really want to know what my sons have done this time, because last time a tattler came in someone had jumped off the fence to the trampoline (the fence did not survive this abuse), someone else was trying to climb up the side of the house to do the same thing, and another peed in the garden.

10. The taps and thuds of a kid touching everything in a public bathroom that should have been condemned.

Does that need an explanation?

There are many, many more sounds that strike fear in heart of a parent—a shoe hitting a fan and smacking the wall, the shattering of a plate, "Where are my shoes?", whispers that probably mean the same thing as silence and excessive laughter—but I just heard someone say, "You're gonna pay for that," and I've run out of time to expound upon the sounds of child-raising.

Sometimes it's better to walk around the house with a giant set of noise-canceling headphones. Who can blame you for not hearing everything when parental sanity's on the line?

When the Summertime Blues Come Calling

Since our first son started school five years ago, Husband and I have come to equate summers with looser time constraints, creative projects our sons will complain about doing (one of these days they'll think it's cool…maybe), and the supreme enjoyment of family togetherness. Boys have the wide open space of a day to do whatever it is their hearts wish (usually that's complaining about how they're so bored), with few requirements beyond chores, tidying up, and daily reading time.

The problem is that, right around August, we all start singing the summertime blues.

It's not just because it's so hot here in South Texas (105 on a good day). It's also because we get a little tired of each other.

The last few years have been tight budget-wise as Husband and I have worked relentlessly to build businesses from the ground up with a bunch of crazy children interrupting us at inopportune times. That means we haven't been able to justify the expense of extra trips or special activities, which means we've mostly stayed around the house, all cooped up inside together, because if you venture out, you disintegrate.

You can measure how tired of each other we are by the

number of arguments that happen in the course of a day and the volume of our voices during those arguments. Parents are short with children, children are short with each other, no one listens to anyone anymore. We live in a relatively small house, so there aren't many places to hide from each other.

One of my sons, the one who loves the Great Outdoors, takes refuge outside. He'd probably sleep outside if we let him—but, again, the danger of disintegration looms. Another of my sons closes himself in the garage, which is a playroom of sorts and has become exponentially messier as he's spent more time there (he insists it isn't him). Another two with identical faces are usually sent outside to play on the trampoline and talk about how unfair it is that they have to play outside on their trampoline and their swing set and in their wooden clubhouse all the time.

I haven't yet found an adequate hiding place. I've tried the laundry room, the library, the game closet, my bedroom, my closet, and my bathroom. When I huddled in the shower once, one of my sons came in and announced, "You're way too big to hide, Mama. We'll always find you." I tried not to take offense.

No solace for me in the summer.

Here are some things that have begun to crawl under my skin as we close out our seemingly endless summer.

1. The complaining

I'm not just talking about me. I try hard to have a good attitude about everything, but when you have six children talking all over each other and trying to tell you a story they made up or, in intricate detail, this dream they had last night while, at the same time, two of them are whining that they're starving and why can't you just get breakfast on the table while another is moaning about how he doesn't even like what you're cooking, even though he doesn't know what it is (you're not even sure), it's hard not to complain. Complainers beget complainers.

I've started a complaint jar, where they can now write their complaints down for Husband and me to read later, but, you know, it takes way more effort to write them down, so my sons will typically just close their mouths instead. Which was the point.

2. The heat

It is ridiculously hot in South Texas this time of year. It's so hot that my sons will go outside with the full intention of playing in the Great Outdoors for the rest of the afternoon, but they'll come inside half an hour later with blood-red faces, gasping about how it's too hot to play outside. You know it's hot when kids actually notice the temperature.

It's not unusual for me to get weather notifications about how the heat index is off the charts, which means it's dangerous to play outside for any length of time. No one feels like a good mother when she pushes her children out into a heat that would make her cry if all her tears hadn't dried up on contact with today's oxygen (is there oxygen in this summertime fire? I can't really tell.). So we get a little more family togetherness inside the house. Just what I always wanted.

3. The mess

My sons don't put anything away. We recently had almost a whole week without our children, because Husband and I needed to do some organization work that is impossible with kids underfoot. The house was immaculate when they returned home—and ten minutes later, in their excitement at the new impressive organization, they'd made a grand mess of things. Honestly, I'm surprised we even got ten minutes.

The other day, I told my ten-year-old, who was this week responsible for cleaning up the dining room, which includes an art table, "No one gets to use the paints anymore."

"Why not?" he said.

"Because you used them five days ago, and they're still out."

"But Daddy's the one who got them out," he said.

And therein lies the problem. My sons operate on "Whoever got it out has to put it away," instead of "Whoever was the last one using this has to put it away." They see no fault in this logic, mostly because it benefits them. It doesn't benefit them any longer. I've been quietly amassing points for every item they leave out, and at the end of the month, when they have their allowance payout, my mom will be able to hear the explosion of disbelief from one hundred thirty-two miles away.

4. The noise

Six boys, as you might imagine, can make a whole lot of noise. Sometimes I can't even hear myself think because of all the voices competing to be heard. The noise continues to steadily build all summer, because as they get tired of family togetherness, they start fighting more, which raises voices and word count, both.

I'm an introvert living in the middle of a zoo.

5. All the lights burning

Every time I come into an empty room, the light is blazing. The other night the last of four lightbulbs burned out in my sons' bathroom. Based on the number of times I have found that bathroom light left on, it made sense. So I left them in the dark for a while. And then, when I remembered that boys already have enough trouble getting excrement in the toilet and not everywhere else, I went with LED lightbulbs.

They're still blazing every time I pass, because my sons are under the mistaken impression that they live with a light fairy who follows happily behind them and turns off the lights *for* them so their little muscles don't have to expend the extra effort. And this fairy used to exist, but no longer. Now I just put another mark on the Allowance Subtractions list. They'll likely be paying the entire electricity bill this month.

6. The extra pounds

You're supposed to lose weight for the summer (according to the ridiculous societal standards for women), but I did the opposite. Why? See all the above.

School starts in another two weeks, and I will be glad to return to the regular routine and a more structured way of life. I thrive on routines and predictability.

Of course I will miss my sons when they return to school. These summers aren't endless; my sons are fast growing up and will soon look for any opportunity to be away from home.

So, for now, I will bask in the requests—not requests for

something to drink or more screen time or a dinner that tastes better. I will bask in the requests to sit on my lap or read another story or spend a little extra time coloring a picture with them. And when those requests come, I will allow myself to get carried away—start thinking that I could do this all year, maybe I should homeschool, I could get used to this ever-present chaos. Because it won't take long for the next slap-fight to break out and shake me out of my sentimentality.

There's nothing like the summertime blues to drive you crazy and fill your memory bank all at the same time.

The Many Ways Parenting Has Changed in Modern Times

Parenting sure has changed since I was a kid. My parents didn't know nearly as much as I know—about neurology, psychology, and child development. I am armed with much more information than they ever had. And while knowing all of these important pieces of emotional intelligence and healthy expression and just-right expectations for the behavior of my children, this knowledge also puts much more pressure on parents to get things right—we have no excuse.

I am not a big fan of the kind of thinking that says, "Well, this is what *my* parents did, and I turned out just fine." I believe (and this is a deep core parenting philosophy) that we actually need to give good consideration to those things our parents did and assess whether they were more harmful than beneficial. Sometimes we don't see the truth of it until we sit with memories for a while. Our kids deserve our contemplation, which is why I do it regularly.

I also believe that our kids deserve to have parents who don't feel constant pressure to be perfect all the time. Parenting under pressure means we're not parenting to our full potential. Parenting with freedom allows us to unfold into the kind of parenting that fits us best and benefits our children, too.

We have to strike the balance between the two, and though balance has never been my strong point (just ask my stairs), here are some things I've been contemplating about my own childhood.

1. After-school choices

Today, parents will keep their kids in after-school care until they're in middle school. Husband and I work from home, so we've never had to utilize after-school care—except in the persons of ourselves. But I still tremble a little when I think about leaving my fourth grader "home alone" (which is really "unsupervised," since I'm up in my bedroom, working) from the time he gets out of school at 3:15 to the time I'm finished with work at 5:30.

When I was a kid, however, the choices were latch-key or…latch-key. When I was nine years old, in the same grade as my son, I was already staying home alone because my mother was a single mom (she wasn't divorced yet, but my father wasn't around) and worked to support us. We didn't have a lot in the house—some toys in our room, which didn't appeal to us during our home-alone time; a TV in the living room; and a basement we were afraid of visiting because of all the sounds that creeped out from under the closed door. My mother told us to lock the doors, don't answer the phone or the door, and don't go outside. She also gave us a phone number we could call for emergencies, which we would abuse with crises like, "She hit me," and "He's looking at me and won't stop." If we'd had an actual fire, I don't think our mother would have answered the phone again. Good thing we didn't.

There were no after-school programs at schools, no affordable childcare, no babysitters at the ready (or at least those who would fit into a budget), so this was the only choice for us. My siblings and I survived that time, and we learned discipline and responsibility and how to make a pot of tea and a piece of toast.

2. Dinner choices

Growing up, dinner had few choices. My mother didn't like cooking, so we had a constant cycle of French fries, fish sticks, and macaroni and cheese. Sometimes we had hamburger helper or spaghetti. Sometimes she'd throw in a salad. The genius of it was that these were all foods my brother and sister and I could cook ourselves.

In my household, on the other hand, everything is organic and from scratch. Parents today (or a lot of them anyway) feel badly if we're not providing our kids with the healthiest nourishment around. I realized the other day that my ten-year-old son didn't even know how to make pasta. I fixed that very quickly, and now he's responsible for cooking dinner for us every Wednesday.

3. Dessert

Maybe it's an erroneous memory, but it seems like I remember having ice cream often in my childhood home—rocky road or mint chocolate chip or plain vanilla with a little chocolate syrup (or a lot, if you were my sister who wasn't great at squeezing the bottle) poured on top. Sometimes, when it was in stock, I would sneak ice cream for breakfast. I don't think I ever actually managed to sneak it. My mother knew everything.

Now my kids only get dessert for special occasions, like Halloween or Thanksgiving or birthday parties, because sugar. This is a regular argument in our house. My sons are adamantly clear that we should have dessert every day. And I don't have the heart to tell them that the real reason we don't is because their mother is weak when it comes to sweets.

4. TV viewing parameters and boundaries

There were none in my childhood home. When my brother came home from school, he would start Nintendo before he'd even checked whether he had homework (I'm pretty sure he knew; he just didn't care). He wouldn't stop until dinner started. If my sister or I got home before him (and we tried many times), she would turn on the TV while I sat on the couch with a self-satisfied smile (because beating my brother was rare) and a book.

Now Husband and I monitor our kids' screen time like it's a medical necessity (isn't it? I don't really know anymore. If I hear my kids say "But all my friends get to play as long as they want" one more time, I might have a medical necessity on my hands).

5. Medical care

If we weren't dying, we didn't go to the doctor.

Yeah, that's pretty much stayed the same.

6. Hygiene

In my childhood home, we had a bathroom dance—we only lived in places that had one bathroom, which meant we had to take turns. When it was my turn, I'd have about five minutes to wash in the bath, because my brother took way longer and didn't leave much time for the rest of us. My mom made us bathe every day.

My kids have their own bath, separate from Husband's and mine (and thank goodness for that!). They only bathe every other day.

7. Morning routine

My mother worked, so my brother and sister and I were on our own. We were expected to fix our own breakfast, gather all our things, and get to the bus stop on time. If you missed the bus—tough luck. Find your own ride or walk.

Every morning, I spend fifteen minutes signing folders to acknowledge that my kids have done their homework (even though I don't really have a clue) and that I've seen the way they behaved in class yesterday. I help them pack up and walk them to school. If they are running late to school, I drive them—because school today reflects not on children but on parents. Or maybe that's just my perception.

Still, teaching kids autonomy in a world where folders need signing and kids get in trouble if parents don't sign them is maybe a little much.

8. Weekends

The protocol for my weekends as a kid was this: You're on your own, kid. Sometimes my mom would work weekends when she needed a little extra cash. But mostly it was her time to rest and relax from the demands of single parenting and working more than should have been asked of one person.

Weekends with my sons include Family Fun Days, trips to

the library, and all sorts of activity-based things, because sitting still feels, in today's parenting world, like a crime.

What I conclude from looking back at my childhood and comparing it to my sons' childhoods is this: We can learn, as parents, to take it a little easier, let ourselves off the hook every now and then, cut ourselves some slack. I survived my childhood just fine, the perpetual eye twitch and ever-present anxiety notwithstanding.

This weekend, I think I'll put my feet up and bury my face in a book.

KIDS MAKE THE WORLD... INTERESTING

Warning Labels that Should Come with Children

You know what would make my life so much easier (besides a soundproof plexiglass divider between the front and back seats of my minivan, that is)? If my kids woke up with a warning label plastered to their backs, or, better yet, their faces (I've been known to miss some things when I'm looking—but a warning label on their foreheads? I'd have a hard time missing that).

Why a warning label? So I'd be well prepared for the completely different human beings who crawled out of their beds this morning. So I'd know that yesterday's angel is going to be today's demon or that yesterday's demon is going to be today's heroic angel of the family. So I'd be able to adjust my expectations accordingly.

A heads-up about that would be nice, because being blindsided at 6 a.m. is definitely not on my list of favorite things in the world.

Here are some warning labels that might come in handy.

Caution: Contents are explosive.

I would love to have this warning label on the mornings when one of my kids wakes up with a stomach virus that's been hanging out in their kindergarten classroom and is now, unbeknownst to me, hanging out in their belly, which will soon empty out onto the floor, the stuffed animals decorating that floor, and my feet. This label would save me time, effort, and the inconvenience of gagging every time I think about vomit on my feet (Did I get it all off? Do I want to know?). It would be really great to know that their contents are explosive, or close to it, so I can make sure I don't feed them Annie's Cheddar Bunnies and tomatoes, both of which will stain the entire interior of the car when they explode.

Also, it would be nice to know when the normally compliant child is feeling especially explosive emotionally so we don't let down our guard and think today is going to be an easy day and we are awesome parents (experience has bruised my ego enough to avoid the latter thinking fallacy). I would like to be prepared for the rare times he is explosive, which usually happens when he's told, no, he can't have another snack, because he just ate fifteen mandarin oranges in as many minutes. Actually, I guess that's easy enough to assume; all my sons get pretty explosive if they have to go more than twelve minutes without food. I'm starving them, I'm the meanest mom ever, when they grow up they will eat all the things at all hours of all the days.

My sons, or at least some of them, get explosive when they come into contact, yet again, with the reality that the entire world does not revolve around them. And when they can't quite figure out their state-mandated math homework and I, the queen of college algebra, can't help them, either. And when they don't like my answer to, "Can I finish this real quick" and their tech time's already over. Explosions result from many factors. We are an emotional household.

Warning: Handle with extreme care.

I have an emotionally sensitive child. Usually he does okay, but every now and then, he wakes up and his extreme sensitivity is dialed up to seven hundred on a scale of one to ten. I would like a warning on those days so I could just shut my mouth and not say a word to him, except maybe "I love you," which might be taken the wrong way, because excessive emotionality is not the most rational of vices (I am also an Extremely Sensitive Human, so I know this well, but, as is usually the case, I find it hard to practice what I preach when it comes to dealing with my children.). I would avoid looking at him. Or maybe just go back to bed, because I'm not going to come close to winning on a day when sensitivity is off the rating scale.

Babies, I've learned, aren't as fragile as you think they are, but what I've also learned is that the older children get, the more fragile, in certain ways, they become. Their emotional lives are worth cultivating with care. Except for the times they follow you into the bathroom crying about how you shouldn't be reading a book on the toilet while they're trying to tell you something important and you say you can't really understand them because they have too much nose in their mouth. It's hard to care about the emotional side of things when there's too much nose in their mouth.

Well, there's always tomorrow. Unless it's another day I could have used a warning label.

Warning: Keep all hands and feet inside the ride at all times.

Anytime I'm around my children, my hands and fingers, and, also, my toes and feet, are in grave danger. Also my back. And my neck. And pretty much any place on my body that could get elbowed or rammed or stepped on (you'd be surprised how many there are; age has done its stretching work magnificently).

My sons seem to think Husband and I are human jungle gyms, and any time I stretch out on the floor to attempt some knee push-ups that my arms are too weak to properly perform, they'll jump on top of me, as though, because I'm failing at lifting my own weight, I'll suddenly be strong enough to lift mine *and* theirs, too.

This is why I never do pushups anymore. It's not because I hate them. Maybe.

Danger: High voltage.

There is so much energy pulsing in the bodies of my sons. If I could bottle up half of it and inhale that tincture every other minute, I would still need a miracle to keep up. As it is right now, my sons are always about two hundred steps ahead of me. I'm pretty slow, to be honest. Not as quick on my feet as I used to be back when I played third base in softball. But every time those wrecking balls come hurtling toward me, I do cringe a little, like I used to when someone hit a grounder to third. So at least there's that reminding me of the great I used to be.

I feel like someone should have warned me how much

voltage a boy would have on a life. I've been violently shocked into movement I didn't even necessarily need. I mean, I'll do my interval training and my running-five-miles any day of the week, but trying to chase a four-year-old because he wants to sword fight his brother with the shovel his daddy left out? No thanks.

Danger: Heavy object, lift with care.

This warning would have been a good one for Husband to heed. Every other day he's injuring his back, because he offers to put the nine-year-old, who can walk just fine, on his shoulders, which he used to do all the time five years ago—when sixty-five pounds was a mere thirty-eight pounds—and he forgets that the nine-year-old is now all legs and muscle. Kids are heavier than they look, especially boys. Our pediatrician used to call our babies "solid." They were born with muscle. I kid you not. When the five-year-old was two, he walked out of the bathroom naked, and every muscle on his back quivered. We have a video to prove it. Husband and I were both jealous. The only quivering our bodies see is the bouncing of our extra flesh.

Caution: Adult supervision is recommended.

Well, no kidding. Of course adult supervision is recommended. They're kids, after all.

But I guess I thought that sometimes I might be able to close my eyes for a short five minutes and I wouldn't have to worry about the three pounds of strawberries in the refrigerator getting eaten—or, more accurately, inhaled—before I woke up again. I guess I thought I could "take a minute" in my room without the cabinets getting decorated with permanent marker my twins were hoarding somewhere still unknown (I shudder writing these words). I guess I thought I could actually close the door when I went to the bathroom without a kid running out of the house with a steak knife to "cut a carrot" that is invisible.

But no. Adult supervision is recommended at ALL times. At least until my sons are fifteen or so. And even then, it's debatable whether supervision can loosen its grip.

Better just get used to peeing with the door open.

This is not, by any means, an exhaustive list of the warning labels that should come with children. Believe me, there are so many more. But there's only so much time in a day to write before I have to peek my head out of my room and make sure no one's burned the house down yet. I'm kidding. I never write on my kid-shift. Husband takes care of the kids when I write.

Which, come to think of it, is actually no guarantee that the house won't burn down, but, hey, he knows what he's doing. So I'll let him do it.

Kids Believe Some of the Most Outrageous Things

Kids have amazing imaginations. They will listen to a story and ask to see the pictures, even though there are no pictures to see, because their brains are constantly working out what they're seeing in the words. They're able to imagine things like a cross between Batman and SpongeBob Square Pants, which we'll call Squatman for our purposes, and they're capable of imagining what they'd like for dinner instead of this nasty spaghetti squash, and they can efficiently imagine a better world without parents like us telling them to go to bed and put those LEGO constructions away and eat all their vegetables.

But sometimes their imaginations can come back to bite them. Say, when they're in trouble or are about to be in trouble, but they're locked in an erroneous belief system and thus do not take the necessary precautions to avoid said trouble.

Here are some of the most outrageous things that kids believe:

1. My parents will never find out.

Every day, when I lay down my twins for their naps, I post up right outside their room, mostly because they cannot be trusted, even at four years old, to be in their room by themselves. Sure, we've cleared it of everything but beds and blankets and pillows, but I tried it out last week—leaving them alone for nap time, I mean—because Husband and I were trying to design a book cover for a new book release, and they managed to pile their blankets and pillows on the floor of their closet, and, even though all the clothes are hung fifteen feet from the floor, pulled down all their brother's twelve-month clothes and tried to squeeze into every shirt—for fun.

What I've noticed about these two is they believe that if I'm not in the room with them, I'll never know what they've done. Forget the pile of clothes strewn all over the floor; I'll probably disregard that—they do.

If I so happen to leave my post for a minute, because I've finished a passage of the book I wanted to read and I'm going to fetch another one, they will sneak on silent feet out of their room and into their older brother's room. They won't even have the foresight to shut the door, so when I come back, there they are standing by their oldest brother's desk, next to the forbidden art supplies he got for Christmas. They'll look at me like a deer mesmerized by headlights and go completely motionless, as if I won't be able to see them if they just stand still enough.

Kids believe that if their parents are not right there with them, we'll never know what they've done. Well, they're wrong. I know every time, kids. I know when you peel paint off your walls and stuff it behind your bed. I know when you've had a couple of extra treats, even though you tried to hide the wrappers underneath some old cucumber shavings. I know when you "accidentally" bring LEGOs into your room, even though it's forbidden and you haven't made a sound (so you think).

I know when you sit down and stand up and when you're awake and asleep. I'm like Santa Claus on steroids. I have eyes everywhere. Don't even think about it.

2. If I can't see a parent, a parent can't see me.

So many times have I proven this wrong, and so many times have they still believed in the possibility. I suppose it speaks to strong convictions, which will benefit them later. For now, it's not an asset.

Here's a regular occurrence: my twins are in their room. I'm sitting right outside their door, but I'm hidden behind the crib, which means they can't see me. So they think that means I can't see them. I get a kick out of this, because they're usually headed into the bathroom to pick up their earlier search for another tube of that yummy mint toothpaste they ate this morning, and they're so intent on this purpose that they don't even glance my way. I'll let them tiptoe all the way out of their room, still oblivious to my body, flattened against a wall, and when they're dead even with me, I'll call out their name. They'll startle and go screaming back to their room and then yell at me for scaring them.

Poor kids.

It's great entertainment.

I mean, it's a great natural consequence. You do what you gotta do. And maybe, sometimes, you get to have a little fun with it.

3. Even though we've done the same thing every night

for the last eight years of my life, tonight is probably different.

This is ridiculously ridiculous. I still can't wrap my head around it.

We run our house on a strict routine; we have to in order to function successfully as a family. Every single night we have dinner time and after-dinner-chores time and bath time and story time and Mama-reading-a-chapter-book-out-loud time and silent reading time and prayer time and brush teeth time and snuggle time and then, at last, bedtime. We have done this routine almost every night since the oldest slipped into the world fighting like he would fight most days of his life: fiercely.

Still my sons seem to think that somewhere in this standard routine is a jump-on-the-couches-naked time and a play-freeze-tag-in-the-house time and a throw-books-in-the-air time.

Nope. That's never been a part of the routine, kids. Get back in your chairs, open your books, and read.

4. If I complain/scream/whine enough, I'll get exactly what I want.

You know what complaining/screaming/whining actually makes me want to do? It makes me want to take away anything I've ever given my kid in the first place (life being the exception, of course). Doing it longer or louder or more annoyingly is only going to guarantee that my carefully controlled crazy will come unhinged. And I can't be held responsible for whatever happens when my carefully controlled crazy comes unhinged.

Whoops. Sorry I just threw away all your LEGO pieces. You were complaining too much about how all your friends have the newest Minecraft set and how you really think, because you're so great at school and all, that you should be able to get the new one, too, and can I take you to the store right this minute so you can buy the latest ninety-dollar set?

Whining/screaming/complaining has never, does not, and will never work.

5. Transforming into Boneless Puddle means I'll get to stay at the park longer.

"Let me stay at the park" could be replaced by anything a kid wants. It's just that the park experience happened more recently than anything else.

Husband and I get these wild ideas every now and then—like, "Hey, let's have a picnic out at the park so the boys can play after they're done eating." Which ends up more like, "Hey, let's have a picnic out at the park so we can drag one of the boys kicking and screaming away from the slide he wanted to go down one more time."

With six sons, it's highly probable that, come closing time, I'll have at least one of them who's not ready to leave the park. It doesn't matter if we're going home to eat dinner or if we're going to another friend's house for a playdate or if we're doing something fun, like seeing a movie, and we'll be late if we don't leave right this minute. They're not ready to leave, ever, so one (or more) of them will collapse into an astonishingly good performance of Boneless Puddle, at which time their daddy or I will drag them to the car, trying to ignore the way the asphalt is tearing at their jeans—not so much because we're concerned about scraping their knees (natural consequences and all) but because those jeans still have to make it through one more kid.

Yes. I'm talking about my twins, once again.

What transforming into Boneless Puddle really means is that I get to work on my strength training for a second time today, and, also, we're not coming to the park again for at least a year.

6. That can't hurt me.

There are so many times this erroneous belief has seized my sons by the shoulders and shaken them until their teeth fall out (sometimes literally). But the one that stands out most, right now, today, is when my boys are sliding head-first down our stairs, just for the fun of it. When the stairs beat their rib cages, they shout their laughter, and they can't stop. It's the most hilarious thing ever, apparently, to have a rounded bit of wood jab into their internal organs and bruise them from the inside out. I watch this, horrified, from the bottom of the stairs as they come jolting toward me. Someone is going to break something, but they are disturbingly unafraid, as is the case for many, many things.

They have no idea how much it will hurt if this little slide goes wrong. I'm relatively certain boys are not programmed to think about trivialities like that.

This fallacious belief also drives them to play bounce-wrestling games on the trampoline and ride bikes without helmets and soar down our cul-de-sac hill lying flat on a weaving skateboard.

And last but not least...
7. Vacuum cleaners can suck you up.

When our oldest son was about three years old, he was terrified of our vacuum cleaner. He would have nightmares and tell us all about them. In his nightmares, there was such thing as a vacuum cleaner that could suck up a person, and he carried around an irrational fear that this vacuum cleaner would come into his room in the middle of the night and suck him up inside it. The vacuum cleaner could not be anywhere near his bedroom or he would spend sixteen hours awake instead of sleeping, and then the next day he'd be delightfully delightful. We could not turn on the vacuum cleaner without one parent being very near him so that he could clutch an arm or a leg or whatever appendage was closest to him. Ear, eye, lips. Didn't matter. As long as he was assured that someone was there protecting him.

I remember being more terrified of escalators than a vacuum cleaner, but maybe that's just proof that I need to get my kids out of the house more often.

Fortunately, as kids grow older, they give up these outrageous beliefs. They learn better. They do better.

It's cute while it lasts. Or something like that.

The Madness of Traveling with Children

Summertime is a time of travel, or at least we like—and try—to make it so in the Toalson home. We idealistically plan those Great American Road Trips with seeming regularity—forgetting all about the disasters that happened last time.

Our Great American Road Trip is typically three hours down the road, to see the kids' grandparents (my mother and stepfather). One thing we can always count on during these trips is the never-ending cadence of "Are we almost there?" and "How much longer until we're there?" We try always to come up with creative ways we might be able to answer these questions. Turns out there are a lot. Take, for example, some of our recent answers: "I'm sorry, did you say, 'Are we Aldous Clare?' No, we are not." "Every time you ask we get farther away. It's like a time traveler's nightmare." "I think it might be the next Ice Age before we're there; what do you think?" Our sons never think these answers are as funny as we do, but it's not for them; it's for us.

But I'm getting way ahead of myself, probably because my eye is still twitching from the last trip.

The trip there is nothing compared to the circus that happens before we even get in the car.

Here's what taking a trip with children looks like in my house:

The packing list

Husband and I are attempting (mostly catastrophically) to teach our sons to pack for themselves. After all, we won't always be there for them to lean on. Packing for yourself gives you agency, makes you feel proud you've done something for yourself.

Or so we tell them. Our sons look at us like we've just told them all the food in the house is gone and now they have to hunt for their own.

Teaching kids anything is a difficult endeavor. Not only does it take twice as long for them to do it, at least until they get good at whatever it is (if they ever do; the nine-year-old still takes an hour to sweep the kitchen floor to parental standards), but it also requires extra time on the part of a parent. Teaching requires time.

On the last trip, my eight-year-old packed for himself but forgot extra underwear. He had only the pair he was wearing. He wore them inside out and backwards before washing them, but, hey, at least he was the eco-friendly kid on that trip.

My packing list

I'm not really sure why I make my own packing list; I'm usually so concerned that my sons have everything *they* need that I'll end up forgetting something important anyway—like my toothbrush or my hair brush or, most recently, a bra that is not a sports bra. Lists don't help when you've forgotten what you marked off because one of your sons was whining about how he can't find any socks and you just did laundry yesterday.

What was I going to put in my suitcase? It probably wasn't important (it always is).

Toward the end of my list, I start getting lazy and don't mark anything off, which ends in chaos, confusion, and regret for the item or items I cannot live without. I'll just have to use Husband's deodorant, I guess.

The lights left blazing

When it's time to pack up and head down the road, I'm the official Turn Off the Lights person. This is not a democratically voted position; it is a self-appointed one. However. Once I've turned off all the lights left blazing, I will go out to the car and get myself situated, which means it's the perfect time for a boy to forget something important—a book he wanted to bring, perhaps—and return inside the house, leaving a trail of lights behind him. So I must then unbuckle and return inside the house to turn off all the lights I already turned off.

I would like to retire from this job as soon as possible. Someone please tell me how they successfully trained their sons to turn off lights.

"I need a drink"

On the one hand, you don't want to give your kids a lot of liquid that will require stops; I don't like stopping at gas stations because they're dirty and it's a half hour detour because of the clowns with whom I'm traveling. I would rather not have a boy announce to me that he stuck his hand in the toilet just to see what the water felt like—after flushing the toilet but also, alas, after washing his hands.

But once everyone gets in the car, someone will always, like a pre-programmed clock, shout out, "I'm thirsty. I need a drink." Thirsty is contagious, and everyone now needs drinks (especially Mama and Daddy).

On the other hand, I don't want my sons dehydrated. But I've learned my lesson the hard way: rather than let them fill up a large container of water that they'll drink in the next five minutes, I return inside the house and fill up a small lidded container from which I'll let them all sip and then collect to keep up front with me for intermittent distribution throughout the trip.

You live, you learn.

Shoes, shoes, shoes

It is no surprise that when it's time to leave, half my children can't find their shoes. We're going to my mom's, so they can wear one tennis shoe and one flip flip. I don't care.

The details

If we're going somewhere that is not my mom's house, we will most likely be missing significant details. This is typically because Husband did the planning, and Husband is not all that great at collecting details. He's more of a big-picture guy—that's why he's banned from Packing Inspection (which is what I call making sure our sons have what they need). And by the time we're leaving, I'm all detailed-out. Apparently there is a cognitive limit to how many details one can hold in one's brain in a day.

"Where are we going?" he'll say.

"I have no idea," I'll say. "Just drive."

We'll figure out the details later. The sooner we leave the driveway, the less likely another boy will climb out of the car into which I have herded them.

Even though it's quite a production to pull off a successful vacation with so many children and even though vacation is not really vacation when young kids are involved, we're grateful we've road tripped every single time, at least by the time we get back home and memory—nostalgia—has glossed over what remains of the frustration, bedlam, and bribes it required to leave our house in the first place. Husband and I always end idealistically, thinking what fun the next trip will be and forgetting altogether the circus that marks departure.

It's better that way.

Rules I Never Thought I'd Have to Institute

I am daily astonished by the things I have to call "rules" in my house—things you'd think are merely common sense. I took what I thought was common sense for granted. Excessively so. It seems, however, that my sons have come standard with pretty much zero ability to use the predictive part of their brain: as in, predicting future consequences, predicting outcomes, predicting parental response.

I have high hopes that they will develop this necessary art as they grow.

But for now, here are some surprising rules I never thought I'd have to put in place (but was proven egregiously wrong—hence the new entries in our Family Playbook):

1. Drinking cups should be and will be used as drinking cups.

This is a no-brainer, right? Why would anyone think that drinking cups should be used for anything other than drinking? Well, that's a good question, and I encourage you to ask it of my sons the next time you see them. They have transformed drinking cups into mud pie containers, a snail collecting contraption, a shovel with which to dig a hole in the backyard that I will fall into in my haste to rescue the drinking cups that should be used as drinking cups. They've used them for freezing their science experiments, which they line up on shelves in our freezer (more on that later, because of course it required a rule); for housing a gigantic serving of rolled oats that aren't cooked and then adding milk, which they'll try even though they already know they don't like this bland recipe and then leave by the kitchen sink to sour and expand; for collecting cars they want to hide from their other brothers.

We have lost so many cups to their creative innovation that they are currently drinking from bowls, like the cat.

As of today, a clarification has been added to this rule: Drinking cups should only be used for drinking beverages that are approved for consumption by humans. I won't tell you why this clarification was added but will only say that with four-year-old twins, you just never know what you'll get. One of them once drank old rain water from a collecting tank that also contained a dead fly, a drowned roly poly, and some sort of mildewed or diseased leaf. That's why they never get sick, by the way. Great immune systems. We should take a page from the Toalson Twins' Handbook.

Or not.

2. Excrement belongs in the toilet.

No, you may not pee off the top of the van. No, you may not pee on your brother's head or in the schoolyard or right out in the open at church. No, you may not shed your pants in the neighborhood park and do your business.

I know they have an easy and convenient way to take care of business, because they're boys, but come on. Who raised these boys? Savages.

3. You must be wearing underwear to _____ .

I chose a blank to finish this sentence because you would be surprised by the number of things that must be said about the necessity of underwear. You must be wearing underwear to go outside. You must be wearing underwear to sit on my lap. You must be wearing underwear to stand in front of your open window and dance.

I really don't think they streak naked through the house on purpose. I think boys simply love to be naked. They are free and uninhibited, and the world has not yet told them who it would prefer them to be in terms of their bodies. I would like them to retain this innocence, this joy, this love of nakedness.

In moderation, of course. I still won't serve dinner to any naked children.

4. Bath water belongs in the bath tub.

So many rules are obvious and yet incredibly difficult for children to grasp. Husband and I have to tell our sons, constantly—no matter how long they have been taking baths, how many days they have practiced this—to turn off the bath water before it reaches the lip of the tub. We have to tell them not to pour cups of water over the side of the bath tub and onto the floor—those cups are for rinsing soapy heads, not facilitating a flood. We have to tell them not to spray bath water onto the ceiling with bath toys, because it causes mildew (What's mildew? Something that can kill you. Sometimes you have to be a little dramatic to sharpen your point and make them believe it's important. You learn this in the years you're a parent. The explanation will work until they start studying mold and mildew in their science class. I'm banking on the hope that, by then, they'll be too old to think it's fun to spray water from a whale's spout right at the ceiling.).

5. Bedtime is bedtime is bedtime is bedtime is bedtime. Stay in your bed unless there's an emergency.

We have a problem with bedtime, and that problem is the patter of little feet on floors after we've turned out the lights. The problem boils down to this: my sons, even after significant training, still retain a misguided perception of what constitutes an emergency. One will barge into our bedroom to tell us that he lost his library book he was *just reading*. Not an emergency. Another will slink in to say his soccer socks are dirty and he doesn't have any more for tomorrow. He doesn't play soccer, he just likes pulling socks up to his thighs. Not an emergency. Another will tell me that he needs a Band-Aid because he accidentally bit his finger when he was trying to suck off the toothpaste he just emptied onto the counter, likely on purpose. I guess that's a little bit of an emergency—his fingertip is hanging on by a thread—but no one's *dying*.

Bedtime is the hardest part of the day for kids and parents. No child wants to stay in their beds once they've been put there. I understand. But I don't understand enough to let them roam the house once I've said it's bedtime. Get in your bed or it's early lights out tomorrow (also: I wish someone would tell me I had early lights out tomorrow. I could use a night like that.).

6. Some things should only be operated by adults.

(Followed by a list of all the things, added to daily)

Like gas cans, which my twins poured all over themselves and the backyard, in the middle of a Texas heat wave during which it's likely you'll spontaneously combust just walking outside, without the help of gasoline. We were on edge for days, but nothing happened, thankfully.

Plungers should also not be operated by four-year-olds—or six-year-olds or seven-year-olds or nine-year-olds. Only by the parents. This is especially important, because the toilets in my house—at least the ones used by my sons—are rarely ever flushed, and that means when boys decide they will take it upon themselves to plunge the plugged-up toilet, there's more than just toilet water that gets splashed onto the walls.

7. Freezer space is reserved for only frozen *edible* food.

A no-brainer again.

However. My sons use our freezer space for a bowl full of honey, because they want to see what honey does when it's frozen. They use it for a bowl full of honey with a Hot Wheels car stuck in the middle of it, because they want to see what a bowl full of honey with a Hot Wheels car stuck in the middle of it does when it freezes. They use the freezer for a concoction of half milk, half water, and a LEGO mini figure sunk down at the bottom, just to see what happens when they freeze it and defrost it hours (or months) later.

I appreciate this ingenuity on the part of my sons, but I would like a space in which to store the salmon they'll complain about eating for dinner Friday night.

I have to review these rules so often that I'm considering

substituting the Family Playbook for myself so I can, instead of wasting breath, simply point my sons in its direction with the instruction to read the book again. Maybe it would work. Maybe not.

Rules, after all, are made to be "forgotten," which is to say they are made to be broken.

I guess I should have tweaked that philosophy before I had kids.

The Panicked Thoughts of a Parent When a Twin Goes Missing

When my second son was two, he was a wanderer. Once we took him to a carnival at the school he would eventually attend all through his elementary years. None of my sons were in school yet, but we were good friends with a family whose son was in kindergarten. They invited us to attend the carnival with their family, and we thought, "Why not?"

Why not is an enemy of the parental people.

The carnival was targeted specifically toward young children. Most of the booths contained activities and games that young children would love—face painting, dart-throwing (they had very dull tips), a dunking station where, instead of dunking the teacher, kids tried to climb in and dunk themselves (it was the middle of May. I don't blame them.). Older kids—or parents—could run around in giant hamster balls for a thrilling, anxiety-inducing race—or, perhaps, an exercise in radical empathy for those poor hamsters who think they're getting somewhere, only to bounce off a wall and be met with the realization that they are, still, captives. So to speak.

At the time, we had a five-month-old son in a stroller, and we decided to let the eighteen-month-old walk. He was already an easy kid—complaint, sweet, malleable. I pushed the stroller, Husband was supposed to be watching the walker, while our oldest, who was three, held on to the stroller. For a while, all went entirely as expected. But, of course, no outing with children will ever go as expected. There is always a moment where everything falls apart.

That moment, this day, was when the three-year-old ran off with his friends without telling us (this would happen time and time again as he grew older; he is so charmed by independence that he genuinely does not remember his parents need to know such things).

I noticed he was gone almost immediately. "Where's J?" I asked Husband. We looked around. No J anywhere.

"I'll go check by the games," Husband said.

I nodded numbly and then turned back to the stroller. Only one kid remained, buckled. The eighteen-month-old had also disappeared.

Husband looked at me, his eyes wide. "Where's A?"

The problem, really, is that we were in a crowded place where there were, also, hundreds of children who looked like J and A. How could we distinguish between them?

I tried to remember what they were wearing, but the only thing my brain could hold at that moment was all the ways they could die outside of our protection. My mouth went dry. My left arm went numb. My throat felt like someone was karate-chopping it.

The elementary school rammed up against two streets—one that was busier than the other. Husband ran for both of those streets, to make sure our second son hadn't walked back the way we'd come. By this time I'd located J's friends and noted he was with them. I'd informed the parents of these friends that our other free-to-walk son had wandered away, and they offered to keep an eye on my oldest until we found the missing son. As I combed through the crowd of people, my heart hammered in my chest. My sweet, blue-eyed boy would be the perfect child to steal. I hoped no one had taken him.

Fortunately, everything turned out fine. Soon after Husband ran off, a man's voice came over the loudspeaker, saying he had a cute little blue-eyed boy in his arms who was looking for his mother. I sent Husband to retrieve him so no one would connect him and this grievous error to me.

Over the years, this has happened more than once. Not with this particular child but with two other particular children. Our twins.

They have wandered off more times than I care to admit. We finally invested in some child leashes and now require them to wear them everywhere—even up to check the mail. You'd be surprised how much trouble can be found in two hundred meters.

I've had quite a lot of practice with the panicked thoughts that invade your brain when your kid goes missing. And while the thoughts that invade your brain when one of your *twins* goes missing are not completely unlike those that happen with a singleton, there are some definite differences.

Here's what my headspace looked like on a recent outing to the San Antonio Zoo, when one of my twins wandered off while Husband was talking to some relatives who'd come to visit and I was keeping my eye on four of our six sons. Husband and the relatives were supposed to be watching the twins. I should have known how that would end, but you know what they say about hindsight.

I don't know how long he'd been missing. I just know that my panic was palpable. I could taste it in my mouth.

Thought 1: Oh my God, one is missing.

What am I gonna do? I'm the worst mom ever. The one who's not missing is gonna be scarred for life because he lost his twin—which means, essentially, I've lost them both.

I mean, would it be all that bad? They're three, which means they're pretty much twerps all the time. Which one is missing? Oh, yeah, the one who's been arguing with me all morning. He probably did it on purpose, because he knew it would freak me out. He's the best at being a twerp.

What are you thinking, you terrible mother!

But they wouldn't have two brains for scheming. There's no way one could dismantle the fan without the other partner in crime. How much easier would life be?

Not easier, just different. You wouldn't want that.

Wouldn't I?

He's your kid.

Oh my God! My kid's missing! Breathe!

Thought 2: What if he walked off with someone?

Well, I hope it's someone who's at least a little nice to him. Maybe nicer than I am. Maybe the person will hug him more and be more patient with him when he's arguing and… [go into the wallowing self-deprecating place that says I wasn't a good enough mother, which is why he's now missing]

Wait. I'm an awesome mother. Because this is the kid who told me he hated me just a few minutes ago, and you know what? *I'm still looking for him.*

Lucky kid.

Thought 3: Maybe he's in the lion display.

Our baby is gonna die. And they'll probably also kill the lion, which is sad. People are gonna hate us. They're gonna call us neglectful parents because no one understands how fast it happens.

Who cares what people think? Just find my kid.

Thought 4: I'll never find him in this crowd.

And it's thickening. Someone probably saw how cute he was, or maybe they noticed that we had two who looked exactly the same and they decided we didn't really need two of them and they'd take one off our hands or maybe some religious fanatic thought they were clones and decided to do some testing on one of them…

(Clearly, the mind is not always rational in such cases.)

Thought 5: What if I don't find him?

With this thought come the memories of all the times I said I never wanted twins and I complained (endlessly, sometimes) about how hard they were and I told people, half joking but mostly serious, that they'd never want twins either— WHAT IF I NEVER FIND HIM?

Thought 6: I never should have taken off that leash.

I know better. As soon as they are granted a tiny bit of

freedom, they take it and fling it in our faces.

Thought 7: We shouldn't have come here.

I knew it was a bad idea to come to the zoo on such a crowded day. Crowds just provide more opportunity for everything bad that could happen in the world.

Thought 8: What if he's forever gone?
Thought 9: What if his twin brother never recovers?
Thought 10: What if we all never recover?
Thought 11: What have I done?
Thought 12: Wait. Is that him?

A boy was racing toward us, a look of terror painting his face.

That boy was my son, the missing twin. He was being chased by a zoo employee, who was only trying to get his name so they could page his parents. He barreled into Husband's arms.

Thought 13: THAAAAAANK GOD.
Thought 14: I am so angry I could kill him.

Which would negate this entire thought exchange—so I won't. But I want to.

After countless experiments in "Let's See if They're Old Enough to Walk Without Backpack Leashes," Husband and I have decided to never remove the leashes, at least for the foreseeable future. Welcome to sixth grade, kid. Now that you're at the front door of the school, I'll set you free.

You do what you have to do to keep your kids alive, right?

The Wonder of Dismantling Things: an Empowering Tale

My sons are curious about practically everything. They will try to pull apart anything in the world (spiders and scorpions excepted) to discover for themselves how it works. Curiosity is a great trait to possess—just not when it involves our refrigerator, thanks.

Sometimes I wonder what in the world my kids are thinking when they take things apart. I can see how the inner workings of a piano might seize their interest and make them wonder, almost obsessively, how they might possibly replicate the intricate mechanics and invent an instrument of their own.

I remember, as a kid, watching my brother disassemble a tape recorder, a clock, a bike, and most of our electronic toys. He wasn't limited to electronic toys, though. He once took apart my entire Barbie mansion, which he said was first hit by a tornado and then invaded by his He-Man action figures.

Yeah. Sure.

My sons do the same thing, except they've added to the list a dishwasher (it was an old one we'd replaced, thank goodness), some roller blades, and multiple electronics like old phones and watches. That's not all, either. The list is practically neverending. I just don't feel like rehashing it all; it was slightly traumatic every time I burst into a room and found something else dismantled.

I, too, often wonder how things work, and I'm mesmerized by the inner workings of things, but I don't take it a step further than that. That is to say, I don't take things apart—especially when I know I likely won't be able to put it back together. My frugality always says, "You really want to replace this?"

My sons did not come equipped with this voice, however.

Quite often I try to practice radical empathy and wear their shoes, small as they are, for a few moments of contemplation. I try to imagine how "normal" it is to see a ceiling fan, wonder about its mechanics, and proceed to take it apart.

Not too long ago, we had to replace the ceiling fan in my twins' room because it was hanging by a wire. This was because we foolishly outfitted that room with a bunk bed, thinking it was better to separate them while they slept, so they could develop into their own people. We did not think about how much closer that bunk bed put them to the ceiling fan.

Alas, they could not resist all the fun this promised.

Because Husband and I have had lots of experience with these two and experience has taught us that they would not be able to curb their curiosity about the wire hanging from their ceiling after we relieved it of its ceiling fan, we removed their bunk bed and gave them a double bed instead (which they have also, since, destroyed).

Here's what I imagine my sons are thinking when they see

something that has not yet been taken apart and the inner workings satisfactorily examined:

That looks interesting.

I wonder how it's made.

I think I'll take it apart and see.

It's really a very simple process, because boys are, at their most complicated, pretty simple creatures. All they really need is food, sleep, food again, food to the infinity.

And stimulation in the way of taking things apart.

The other day I braved the tornado of my ten-year-old's bedroom only to find the brand new diffuser taken completely apart—the plug was removed from the back of it, the lid was somewhere I couldn't see, water and essential oil was spilled everywhere. This crime scene wasn't the work of the ten-year-old, however, it was the work of the two-year-old, who hasn't quite figured out how to take things apart to a point where it completely destroys them. He did his best. And all I had to do was clean up water mixed with Peace and Calming and put it back together. It's wasn't so bad.

Later that day, I returned back downstairs after, arguably, too long hiding from chatty boys in my bedroom, and all the couch cushions had been thrown off the couch. They weren't looking for change (we don't carry it), they were looking at the inner workings of a couch. They didn't find anything; no one had thought it a good idea to take out the scissors and cut away the cloth that covered springs. I called that a win.

Still later one of my sons slipped behind the piano to see what was happening there while his brother banged on it—and he nearly lost his hearing. And later still, one of my sons used all his muscles to pull the refrigerator out because it wasn't cooling properly, and he thought he could fix it using the quantum mechanics he likes to read about as a ten-year-old.

Generally, I would encourage this curiosity in my sons. It's a precursor to creativity, and it's good to be curious about how things work. It can also be a little bit dangerous. For example, my twins, before we moved the bunk beds out of their room, were caught trying to figure out how to take the bunk beds apart—while they were in it. This could have resulted in multiple injuries, but they didn't even consider that. This is because boys are also impulsive. They don't think about the consequences of taking something apart while they're in it.

When I caught them, they were underneath the top bunk, unscrewing things as well as they could (it wasn't very well). I watched them for a minute before stepping in.

"What do you think you're doing?" I said.

They both nearly hit their heads they were so startled.

"Nothing," they said at the same time.

"Are you taking your bed apart?" I said.

"Yeah," one said.

"No," the other said.

"While you're in it?" I said.

"Yeah," one said.

"No," the other said.

"What do you think will happen?"

They both shrugged. They didn't think at all about what would happen. They probably don't even *know* what would happen.

I left them to it. Sometimes you have to learn the hard way.

And I'd also seen that they weren't twisting screws at all; their fingers were sweaty. It gave the illusion of screws moving. That bed wasn't coming apart anytime soon, except in their imaginations.

That evening, we saved the bunk beds *and* our curious boys by giving the beds to our older sons, who are hopefully less impulsive.

Hopefully.

Songs that Could Be About The Parent Life

We were driving down the road one night in the place my boys are always the loudest—the van—and a song came on that made me think: *This one's about kids.* Another one came on, and I said to Husband, "Hey, this one's about kids, too."

He looked at me like I was a little crazy, because I hadn't said the first observation aloud, so the "too" was unnecessary, but I pretended not to notice. "This song," I said. "It could be about kids."

Half an hour later, I realized that nearly every song could be applied to my kids.

Because we're creative people, Husband and I then had to sit down and make a list of all the songs that apply to children. There were hundreds. Here are our favorites.

1. "In the Air Tonight," by Phil Collins

There is one particular line in this song that applies much more than the others: "I can feel it coming in the air tonight."

It is handed down in the parenting folklore that kids come with a witching hour. For my kids, this witching hour lasts from about half past four until around seven. My kids are overachievers, like me. The witching hour is, for them, the witching *hours*.

Some nights this witching is much more exaggerated than others. On those nights, you can feel the falling apart nature crackling in the air, like electricity for which you have not paid. It is stolen electricity, but it is coming in the air tonight. Oh, Lord.

Nights when I can feel "it" coming in the air feature kids jumping off top bunks when they're supposed to be sleeping; kids ignoring all instructions and, instead, raising the general level of the cacophony so they don't even have to hear the instructions (where did I put that bullhorn? I'm really missing it right now); and kids roller blading up and down stairs, as though they are daring injury to smack them in the face.

Unfortunately, this stolen electricity crackling through the air does not invigorate parents. In fact, we only want to pull up the covers and pretend what's happening outside our door doesn't exist. But one or the other of us will rise and do what must be done: tame whatever is in the air tonight.

2. "A Hard Day's Night," by the Beatles

Does this one really need an explanation? Isn't every night with children a hard day's night? When does it become easy?

This song is especially appropriate when one of my children is sick with the stomach virus. It will most definitely be a hard day's night, a hard tomorrow's day and night, and likely a hard month's night. We once hung on to the stomach flu for forty wretched retching days. And though the kids could puke and play, once that virus hit me, I could only die. Or nearly so.

3. "I Want to Hold Your Hand," also by the Beatles

I hear this theme song playing when I'm walking my sons to school and everyone wants to hold my hand. I only have two hands. I have five walkers. I need three extra hands (one's in the stroller, so he doesn't usually ask, though he doesn't like to be left out of anything). Plus, I'm pushing a stroller.

What this usually looks like is one mom tripping, every other minute, over four boys who are fighting over who was holding my hand first—and one quiet, uncomplaining child holding the baby's hand instead. He's my favorite today.

Extra limbs would sometimes be nice, except when I think about sleeping. I already don't know what to do with my arms when I sleep. More arms would be problematic.

4. "Eight Days a Week," once again by The Beatles

Every night, when I fall into bed, I feel like I've lived more than one day. I feel like I've lived maybe two or three days. At the end of my week, with the exception of how much actually got done, I feel like I've lived eight days, not seven. This song is highly appropriate for a parent's life.

5. "This is My Fight Song," by Rachel Platten

My kids will fight to the death to take back control of their lives. Husband and I allow them quite a lot of autonomy and opportunities for decision-making, if they are responsible in their decision-making (and responsible doesn't just mean making the decision we would make; we teach them to think critically about what they're considering). However. For strong-willed, opinionated children, I don't think there's ever enough autonomy or decision-making opportunities, at least in their minds.

This fight song starts playing every time one of my sons wants to invite a friend over to our house but his Pokémon cards are displayed in a nice carpet, rather than placed neatly in the holding case. It rings out when they haven't done their homework and they are particularly perturbed that this is a requirement at all; they'd rather play. It blasts its first line the minute my sons say they want to have technology time but they mouthed off ten minutes ago.

I'm pretty good at fighting, fortunately. I knew that high school debate team practice would eventually come in handy someday.

6. "Wrecking Ball," by Miley Cyrus

I will never forget the day I heard my twins out in the backyard singing this song, and I could do nothing but laugh, because, yes, they did come in like a wrecking ball. It is actually quite astounding how much they have destroyed around our house and in our lives. Two days before I heard them singing this song, they had peeled off nearly all the paint on their bedroom walls and left the tiny pieces in a corner of the room for Husband and me to find later. They had chewed on their blinds—the third blinds we've bought for the one window in their room. Now they'll be getting blinds for Christmas, because we're done replacing what we didn't destroy. They had taken jeans with holes in them (and there are many; they're numbers four and five in a line of boys and clothes that have been passed down) and "accidentally" made the holes bigger.

I plan to write a book about all their destruction and, the day they graduate high school, hand it to them when they ask why they don't have any college money like their brothers did.

7. "Dark Horse," by Katy Perry

Are you ready for the perfect storm? Because kids are always ready to deliver.

They will come at you, barreling, like a dark horse, uprooting everything you know and understand about kids, yourself, and life. I hear this song every time I'm pitted in a battle against them and I have to remember how to parent empathetically when I am face to face with a little human being. In those moments I stand at a crossroad: Do I want to be the old person I used to be or the new one who is much more patient and kind and understanding? Do I want to be a bird without a cage or a smaller version that my in-the-moment emotions make me? Do I want to crash or fly?

8. "Can't Feel My Face," by The Weeknd

It's true. They make me smile and laugh so much that sometimes I can't even feel my face when I'm with them. Sometimes it's numb from anger or shock, arguably, but most of the time numbness only follows genuine joy and amusement. Kids make me feel a paradox of emotions, but it's the smiling and laughing that take center stage.

Though many of these songs mean I'm in for a rough time —day, week, month, whatever kids want to make it—hearing them during the moments of my day makes me feel like I'm living the life of a superstar. With less pay, nonexistent makeup (and sometimes showers), and dinner to be cooked, always.

The Astonishing Things Kids Consider Food

The other day I went upstairs to unpack a bag. Husband and I had been out of town for the weekend, and I wanted to be productive while the five-year-old twins were occupied outside, presumably jumping on the trampoline, judging by their shrieks of delight and terror, timed intermittently.

I thought, foolishly, that they'd be jumping for a while.

Little did I know that while I was fully engrossed in the fifteen minutes of unpacking this cursed bag, these two cunning children snuck into the house and smuggled out nine apples. Which they devoured. In fifteen minutes.

When I came back downstairs, I immediately noticed that all the green apples I'd emptied into the fruit bowl had mysteriously disappeared.

Of course I knew what had happened; experience has etched furrows of deduction and logic into my brain. But I wanted to give everyone a chance to confess.

I called all of my sons inside and pointed to the fruit bowl. "What happened to all the green apples?" I said. I wasn't angry or accusing; I simply folded my voice into a cauldron of curiosity.

"I don't know," the eight-year-old said, his eyes fastened on mine. I believed him.

The seven-year-old and the ten-year-old said the same, and I believed them, too. But when I turned my attention to my twins, they avoided looking at me like I had some kind of contagious disease spread through acknowledgment of presence. Which, of course, told me everything I needed to know.

"Did you take the apples?" I asked one of them.

He pointed to his twin brother. "He took four," he said.

"And he took five," his twin brother said. They prefer tattling on each other to confession.

As a natural consequence, their snacks were revoked for the rest of the week (which was only five days). Not having snacks is not gonna kill them, trust me. My sons already eat so much that every time I go through the grocery store line, cashiers ask me if I run a daycare (kind of), if I make a lot of smoothies (sometimes), if I live with a handful of monkeys (why, yes, I do), and many other creative questions.

It might sound cruel to revoke snacks for a whole five days, but when you're five and you consume five apples in one sitting, it logically follows that you have eaten your allotted share of snacks for the next five days. They'll make up for it at dinner. Trust me. Snack time is just one of the many times my sons find an excuse to shove food in their faces. Some kids don't even get snacks. This is a first-world problem.

Plus, there are many other things to eat besides what sits on our counter or hides in our refrigerator. My sons are creative when it comes to filling their bellies. Here's a list of all the things they've tried to eat (and probably will again, now that their snacks are temporarily suspended).

1. A ladybug.

One day one of my sons double-dog-dared his brother to eat a ladybug, and everybody knows that you can't turn down a double-dog-dare. So some unlucky boy swallowed a ladybug and called it a day. He should write a book called *How to Eat Fried Ladybugs*. It would probably be a bestseller.

Most of the world, you might know, consumes insects already, so this really isn't that big a deal. In fact, it might be considered an exotic delicacy. My sons' bug-catching skills will come in handy when the food supply wanes and we need bugs rather than animal meat for our daily protein intake. So thanks for the practice, guys.

2. Dirt.

I don't know what it is about dirt that appeals to my five-year-old twins, but every time they come inside the house after playing outside, it's quite obvious that they've been feasting on it. It's not that they aren't getting the nutrients or minerals they need, which is sometimes the body's reason for craving dirt; we eat healthy around here—and sometimes, as I said before, they eat five apples in one sitting. I think they just like the grainy taste of dirt in their mouth. It's weird, yes, but it's better than eating something else that's brown, like they once did when they were babies.

I would like to wipe that memory clean from my memory palace, but it is lodged into the walls, just like their painting rendezvous with the contents of their diapers is lodged into the fibers of our physical house walls.

3. Grass.

Every now and then one of my sons will come in and say something randomly shocking, like "That grass was really tasty." I'll do a double-take and say, "What was that?" thinking I haven't heard him clearly. But I did, and then I can't even pretend I didn't hear him clearly, because he has another pile of grass in his palm, stretched out to me. I politely decline. Thanks, but no thanks.

4. Raw beans

Since there is no reason you would ever want or need to eat raw beans, I simply pretend not to see it.

5. Pencil erasers

Every pencil that I pull out of the container where we keep them no longer has a working eraser. The other day I put on my Sherlock Holmes cap and observed the teeth marks inflicted all over the pencil body and the twisted metal on its end and the apparent nonexistence of the tiny white or pink cylinder used for correcting mistakes. The only thing I can logically conclude from these observations is that my sons like to eat synthetic rubber. Hope it all comes out all right.

6. LEGO pieces

One day the ten-year-old was building with his LEGO pieces, and he said that they smelled really gross.

"Why would they smell?" I said.

He shrugged. "I don't know."

Two minutes later, I saw one of the five-year-olds with a mouthful of LEGO pieces. He looked like a chipmunk storing up nuts to deposit in his winter hiding place.

"Get those out of your mouth," I said.

"Mmfuolkay," he said.

I don't actually know what he said, but I do know that he bent over the LEGO mat and heaved up LEGO pieces, along with volumes of kid slobber. I felt a little sick to my stomach after watching him, thinking of how many germs were likely living in that LEGO mat. It's no wonder the LEGO pieces smelled.

I'll never build with them again.

7. Gum

We buy sugar-free gum that doesn't contain harmful ingredients because we're annoying health freak parents. What this mostly means is that gum is not cheap. And my sons go through it like candy. We have a rule in our house that they're only allowed to have one piece of gum a day, but someone is breaking this rule, judging by how quickly a bag empties.

But the biggest problem is really what they do with their gum when they're finished chewing it. Sometimes they do what they're supposed to do—spit it in the trash. Other times they'll stick it on the counter while they pour a glass of milk or have another apple, and then they'll conveniently forget they were saving it for later so that the next time I lose my balance and nearly fall, I have the privilege of scraping someone else's gum off my hands. Sometimes the less thoughtful, or perhaps those less efficient at aiming into the trash can, will leave a piece on the floor, where it will either stick to the bottom of an oblivious shoe and be carried all over the house, or our cat will think it's a fun, sticky ball and, if it doesn't stick to his mouth like a cat-man beard, leave this treasure in random, unexpected places so one of us can flatten it beneath our cheeks, a delicious decoration for our derrière.

It's so fun living with kids.

Why don't I outlaw the gum? you might be asking. The answer to that question is simple: gum tricks my sons' stomachs into thinking they're actually eating. Which is important in a house where the grocery bill is already more than you pay for housing. And the teenage Years of the Locusts have not yet arrived. I do what I can.

My point, in all of this, is that boys will try anything once. Sometimes twice or more. Which is great when we're introducing a new exotic vegetable, like eggplant or artichoke or bok choy, all of which they've so far refused, in case you're wondering.

Thanksgiving is coming up. That means my sons will likely be hovering around the stove, peering into the oven, and generally getting underfoot, unaware of how difficult this makes getting the feast on the table in a decent amount of time. So if they do this year what they do every year, I think I'll throw out a few experimental snacks: branches, mud pies, and maybe even a few raw grasshoppers.

Everything's worth trying once for a double-dog-dare (except toilet water. And anything that might drop in toilet water. Please don't.).

Problems We'd Face Living On Our Kids' Planet

Every now and then, my kids get really upset with me and confess that they wish they could live somewhere else—anywhere else but here in this family. I understand; I remember occasionally feeling that way with my own mom and siblings. And when a parent expects you to act like a decent, kind, compassionate human being and do some reading, some writing, some creative work before earning tech time, I'm sure it can get a little annoying to live here in this house. I don't understand that part quite as much as I'd like to; I always had my nose stuck in a book while my brother tried and failed to beat Super Mario Bros. The only thing that could tear me out of a story was the crack of a controller hitting the table on which my brother sat. Frustration abounded in that game, as it apparently abounds in the games my sons play today. Why play something that makes you feel so frustrated? Because it's fun, they say.

They are personifications of paradox.

My ten-year-old the other day wrote in his journal about a fantasy he has wherein he rules the world. He wrote about what the world would be like if he were Supreme Ruler.

Sometimes, for a giggle, I will engage them in these

fantasies. It's fun to imagine you rule the world. But it also shows more clearly how many massive problems we'd face living on a planet of our kids' making. Problems like:

There would be no time.

I'm not talking about the actual measurement of time; we'd be hard-pressed to leave that behind. But kids are notoriously bad at keeping time. My sons will begin their tech time with a timer, and when the timer rings or gongs or whatever they've set it to do, they will say, "No way was that thirty minutes." I will calmly show them that the timer was originally set for thirty minutes and thirty minutes has, indeed, passed. They will argue until they have no more breath to argue, but the evidence does not lie; only the minds do. Intuiting the lost cause (some quicker than others), they'll try to finagle me with seemingly innocent words: "May I just finish this one thing, Mama? It'll only take a minute." I know, by now, that their minute equals about thirty-five of mine.

And therein lies the problem: on a planet run by kids, time would stretch in incomprehensible and (should I say it? Yes, I will) unbearable ways. The Witching Hour could last more hours—even days. I will not be volunteering to inhabit that planet. But thanks for asking.

Bedtime wouldn't be allowed. In fact, there would be absolutely no sleeping time.

Time when children are required to lie in their beds, close their eyes, and enter dreamland would be forbidden on the planet of children. There's too much to do! How dare you even ask! There are magical creatures to make out of LEGOs, there are books to read, there are foam pieces protecting the bars of the trampoline that must be chewed! There are sword fights to conduct, holes to dig, silverware to smuggle out into the backyard. There is tech time!

Sleep is for people who have nothing to do.

On the other hand, if parents had their own planet, I'd be willing to bet most of the time would be spent sleeping or, at the very least, pretending to be sleeping.

It would be too loud to hear anything.

Maybe this is unique to the Toalson home, but my children are loud everywhere they go. We will head out to the streets of our city for a Family Fun Day, and I will tell my sons that even though we're outside, they don't have to screech at one another—but they don't hear me. We will enter a museum, and I will remind them to use their indoor voices, but they've forgotten what that means. We will load up in our car and, besides the ever-present fart cloud hanging around, the one thing I can count on is that Husband and I, all the way in the front seat, will not be able to hear each other talk. I'm still waiting on that police-divider glass to come standard in cars. Any day now.

On the planet of kids, everyone would be talking at once, a conversation would never be finished, and the pitch of it all would resemble the dull roar of wild animals trapped in an elementary school cafeteria.

The entire planet would have to be made of food.

The problem, of course, would be that they would eventually consume the very ground on which they walked (which, arguably, some kids already attempt to do).

My kids are always hungry. Husband and I have to limit snacks in our house, because if we didn't, the world would be gone. They would eat a hole through it, especially if that hole ran through a strawberry patch. My point is, they eat all the time, and even though they have plentiful snacks and seconds and thirds at meals, it is never enough to fill their bellies. They have a hollow leg they're hiding somewhere.

Not to mention, kids don't cook. At least mine don't. I've shown them how to make boiled eggs and toast, how to boil pasta and warm up sauce, and how to pour cereal and milk without turning the kitchen into a disaster area (this skill is still in development). They know how to cut carrots and peel cucumbers and reach for whatever fruit is available. They are fully equipped to feed themselves, but the other day my ten-year-old asked me what would happen if he ate uncooked rice.

"Why?" I said. "Why would you want to eat uncooked rice?"

He shrugged. "Because I don't want to cook it."

Uhhhh…

If kids ruled the world, their planet, by necessity, would have to be made of wholesome, raw food. Which might be kind of awesome, actually.

Everyone would have screen heads.

There is no doubt in my mind that if my kids were left to their own devices and did not have "mean" parents presiding over their time, they would lose themselves in screens. Screens are so much fun, and kids don't have to do much thinking while they're using them. It's the bored child's paradise.

If they had a planet of their own, kids wouldn't even bother with faces; "people" would have screen heads. That way everyone could be entertained all the time and no one would have to think about what was happening outside of screens.

That kind of world makes me shudder.

The planet would be carpeted in LEGOs.

My sons' least favorite thing to clean up in the whole world is LEGO pieces. If they ruled the world, they would never have to; the carpet would be LEGOs. Everyone would wear special shoes and special knee pads and special padded clothing so that if (when) they tripped, they would not puncture a thigh with Batman's left wing.

A planet with a ground made of LEGO pieces would mean not only do kids not have to clean up those LEGOs but also they would get to play and build with LEGOs everywhere they went. They would never be bored again.

In spite of all these unrealistic wishes that comprise a planet ruled by kids, there are some things I would enjoy about living on their planet. Like:

Sweets.

No homework.

Playing all the time.

Money means nothing.

Does the good outweigh the bad? I'm not entirely sure. We can't really know a thing like that until we experience it. So when they discover this planet and take over its rule, maybe I'll see if I can hitch a ride.

Rachel Toalson

For research purposes.

When Cute Kids Become Creepy Kids: a Harrowing Tale

I have some of the scariest kids.

I say this with a sense of deep reverence and appreciation for their sometimes frightful existence. They can pull off scary without even trying, and, with the exception of first thing in the morning, when I roll out of bed, I have to actually give it some concerted effort.

Truth be told, it's not *exactly* accurate to say my kids are scary. It's much more accurate to say they are frightfully surprising. Which can, oftentimes, border on creepy. And may be worse than scary.

I've never much liked surprises. Husband once scared me on purpose by standing right outside my bedroom door, and, when I opened it, there was a wall of a man. That wall regretted his decision when I punched him in the face. It's good to know I have good reflexes, but scaring me is not advisable.

However. My sons *love* to do anything they can to scare me. Generally, when they're trying, their efforts are wasted. One of them stood behind a door the other day, thinking he'd be able to startle me when I opened it, but I could hear him giggling and ended up scaring him, instead. He does not have my fight response; he collapsed onto the floor and played dead

—which entered him into the family folklore of good tales to tell.

Husband has also, on numerous occasions, offered the example of his standing-behind-the-door prank as a cautionary tale. Boys don't listen.

It's when they're not trying, though, that they achieve ultimate creepiness.

There was one night, years ago, that proves my point perfectly. I was sleeping so soundly when a sudden premonition pulled me from that blissful slumber. I sat up in my bed. We keep our room very dark, because it's not good for your brain to see light at night; it gets confused. We're scientific people, so we take these warnings seriously.

Imagine an almost-pitch-black room, a woman sitting up in bed, woken from a very deep sleep, a woman then turning to the side of her bed, a woman coming face-to-face with a form standing two feet away, staring at her.

What would you do?

The form did not speak, nor did he move. But he was there, whites of the eyes gleaming in the dark. For a breathless moment, my imagination went wild: Chucky. The creepy kid from *Pet Sematary*. Any of the monsters in R.L. Stine's Goosebumps books—Slappy in particular.

I wordlessly screeched (it would have been the kind to shatter windows if my voice had actually worked) and landed on top of Husband, who comically bolted out of bed and crashed to the floor, tripping over the old takeout boxes from our Friday order-in date night.

Husband switched on the light, and we saw that tonight's intruder was our third son, three years old at the time. Husband shook his head at me with a "Well, it's a good thing one of us around here doesn't freak out about sleep walkers," but all I can say is at least I'll be ready when Chucky comes.

Husband calmly walked our Creepy Kid back to his bed, while I lay awake, pulling the covers over my face (because the monsters can't get what they can't see!) and hoping Creepy Kid would not come back for me as soon as Husband fell asleep again—which he did, two minutes later. I, on the other hand, lay awake the rest of the night with a heart that nearly hammered through its walls.

Creepy is not a friend of mine.

Another night Husband was out at a workshop he was presenting on some aspect of video production, and I was tasked with Turning Out All the Lights. I am never tasked with this, and there is a good reason. The reason is that there are all sorts of monsters waiting for me in the dark. They are behind me when I'm racing up the stairs, they are at the top of the stairs when I round the corner, they are outside my window.

Darkness and I are incompatible, except when I'm tucked safely in my bed.

If I am ever, for some odd reason, tasked with Turning Out All the Lights, which was assigned to Husband's Responsibility Chart back when we first got married, what typically happens is I will run for my life up the stairs and into my room, which was fully lighted in the preparation (nothing's scarier than running from a monster into the dark of another room). I did this even when I was a kid. My mom could always guess who was the last one up either by the volume of the footsteps (everyone knows the louder you are, the less likely monsters will get you) or by how many lights were left blazing.

This particular night I did not know what time Husband would be returning home. Unfortunately, my children had been downstairs, which means all the lights were left on, because they think we have a Light Fairy who flits around the house flipping off lights after they leave rooms (well, they'd be right about one thing in that sentence). My fear, that night, battled hard with my frugality. I *really* don't like wasting energy —not just because of the cost but because of the environmental implications. I also *really* don't like turning out lights when it's dark.

Frugality and my love of the environment triumphed over my fear. I decided I would brave Turning Out All the Lights. I stretched first. I know what it requires.

I had a good retreat speed going, too. I rounded the corner to come up the stairs, every monster I'd ever read about or seen on the big screen nipping hard at my heels, and who was waiting for me at the top of those stairs?

My identical twin boys. Holding hands. One half-smiling, the other not at all. Just like in *The Shining.*

I screamed all the way up stairs, all the way past them, (I admit: I pushed them out of the way) and all the way to my room, where I slammed the door and tried to remember how to breathe. Fortunately, the sound issuing forth from my mouth was enough to scatter my twins back to their bedroom, too, where they stayed for the rest of the night (I don't really know that last detail for sure, since I did not emerge from my room again. It was too dangerously creepy.).

Sometimes I'll be taking a shower, and a form will move outside the spotted glass, and I'll immediately think I'm probably living a scene from real-life *Psycho*, not the milder product of Robert Albert Bloch's imagination. If that form happens to speak, I'll most likely drop whatever I'm holding on a toe. Hopefully it's not a razor.

Sometimes my kids will cry out in the night, and, when woken from my consistently strange dreams, I won't automatically recognize that the voice calling out belongs to a child. It actually belongs to a werewolf, which is going to devour everyone in my house and turn us into a werewolf family.

One of my sons will snore loudly enough to penetrate my walls, and I'll assume it's the creature from *Stranger Things*, coming to absorb me or whatever it does. One of them will moan, and I'll assume it's a zombie from *The Walking Dead*, which I never actually watched but heard through Husband's headphones. One of them will pound on my door, and I'll assume it's a White Walker with icy blue eyes.

Sometimes I'll be writing in my room, using my standing desk that's not really a standing desk but is actually just a dresser (where I stack books so my computer's elevated to the proper height) with a mirror that provides a little jolt of fear-induced adrenaline when I'm focused on a fictional world and a kid appears in the glass. I usually plug my ears with headphones so I don't have to hear the house falling apart under Husband's command (it falls apart under mine, too; this is not a dig on his parenting), so I don't always hear this ghostly being enter at all. But my eyes see everything, as much as I sometimes wish they didn't.

I try to cover up my startled cry with a shaky "*Whaaaat* are you doing in here?" They see right through it, and they think it's the funniest thing, so, of course, they do it all the time.

The worst, though, is on the mornings when I go downstairs a little earlier than normal. I'm usually lost in my own wonderful world, a world of Kids Aren't Up Yet, because the silent house seems to corroborate that assumption, and I'm looking forward to a morning listening to an audio book instead of listening to the audio of my nine-year-old, who wants to tell me every excruciating detail of the Minecraft ideas he had while he was sleeping.

And then I'll turn on the kitchen light, and there's a figure sitting on a kitchen chair, waiting to kill me.

Not really. It's just a kid. Sitting in the dark. Reading. With no lights on.

My shriek will wake up everyone else in the house. And if it didn't, the front door slamming did (Okay, so my reflexes aren't *always* great. I ran into another sort of danger—the dark morning. But at least I'm proactive in the face of fear.).

Kids are exceedingly cute; there is no way to deny this. My kids are some of the cutest I've ever seen. But they can also become my worst nightmares, bundled up into six creepy containers that tumble about in the dark.

As soon as I let myself forget that, I'll be shivering under the covers of my bed or racing up the stairs past Terror-Inducing Twins, or running for dear life out the front door.

It's better to be on guard.

Side Effects of Parenting: a Scientific Theory

Caution labels are a necessary component to our everyday lives. They help us know what to expect and how to avoid the potential dangers that exist all around us. Take, for example, the words printed on every store-bought cup of coffee: Caution —Hot! or some derivative of that warning. What would we do without it?

Burn ourselves, that's what.

Or, you know, not.

Caution labels are slapped on food, on boxes, on a highly visible sign placed strategically at the entrance to a roller coaster that might risk your life. Just think what it would be like if alcohol didn't come with a warning and we who are parents opened that new bottle of red wine and consumed the entire thing in one sitting without knowing that excessive consumption could impair our ability to think and make decisions and walk and operate machinery. How would our kid's butt get wiped then?

These labels can seem superfluous sometimes (see the coffee cup example above), but the ones I really appreciate are the side effect warnings.

I sure wish my kids came with side effect warnings. They'd

probably look a little like this:

Weight gain

I never used to cave to comfort eating. In fact, I was so strong in college that I went a whole year eating one granola bar a day. Sometimes, if I worked out (and by worked out, I mean ran at least six miles a day, did my weight lifting, and played a little racquetball) I would splurge on one smoothie and one blueberry bagel, hold the cream cheese.

I'm not saying I was healthy because I was anorexic, but my point is, I was strong. I convinced myself I did not need food.

Enter children.

The opposite is now true. I cannot, for the life of me, convince myself that I do not need food. Every pregnancy resulted in at least fifty pounds of weight gain. Every newborn resulted in a mom determined to lose that baby weight. And for the first three, I did. But when my twins were born, I learned that I was not nearly as strong as I thought I was.

Now Husband and I wage a daily war against Eating Your Feelings. One of the kids paints a toilet seat with poop because he didn't feel like wiping, and we Eat Our Feelings. Another kid drops the iPad he wasn't supposed to have and cracks the screen in a billion pieces, so we Eat Our Feelings. Another kid tells us we're the worst parents ever, he's glad he only has nine more years left in our house, he can't wait to leave, he wishes he could have different parents, and we Eat Our Feelings.

Turns out, chocolate *does* make you feel better, which is why I always keep it around.

Loss of memory

Loss of memory is actually only half the story. What kids really do is steal their parents' brains. They're like zombies that are cute. Which is worse, because that makes them much more dangerous. If they were not cute zombies, you would run for your life, but with the cute factor setting up a prodigious obstacle, this fight was over before it began.

Early on my kids stole the control center of my body and shoved it somewhere dark and clever, where it will never absorb the light of day again. Ask me what one plus six is. Go ahead. The answer is: too many nine-year-olds in my house for a sleepover party.

My kids, on the other hand, are excessively smart. I don't say that to brag; they really are. Obnoxiously so. Their brains have figured out how to bore a hole in the wall and cover it with a piece of white peppermint gum, how to stand on a skateboard with roller blades strapped on their feet, and how to construct the kind of elaborate lie that gets them out of trouble for eating two pounds of grapes (but that diarrhea doesn't care about lies).

Brilliant.

I used to be pretty smart. Honestly. But six kids stole pieces of my brain and never gave them back, and now I'm more like a turkey, which the Internet tells me is one of the dumbest animals—and you can always believe what you read on the Internet.

Whether it's because you're trying to balance twenty different lives (even though you only have a handful of kids), or you're trying to keep on top of the school papers, which number in the billions, or you're attempting to maintain everything there is to maintain in a family life, there is way less energy left over for your brain to actually think critically about and consider pretty much anything. That's why most parents, when asked a seemingly simple question, will stare at you with glazed-over eyes. Their brains are black holes, too.

Bladder irregularity

I am intimately familiar with this side effect when I sneeze, when I cough, when someone scares me, and those nights I agree to jump on the trampoline for one son's snuggle time. I should have known better. By the time I come back inside, I have to change my pants.

Here's something they don't tell you in childbirth class: it doesn't matter how many kegels you did before you had your baby. Nothing stops the bladder's flow once you've been ripped apart.

Insanity

Do I need to explain this one?

Oh, okay, I will. Kids are some of the largest and most persistent catalysts to driving a parent bonkers. This is mostly because they wake up completely different people every single day. Just when you think you have them all figured out, that they like blueberries and they don't like cherries, they will show you that you are, in fact, completely clueless about everything when it comes to raising them, including their fruit preferences. And I hear it's even worse when they're teenagers, so at least we have that to look forward to.

It doesn't matter how many kids you have. You are never fully equipped for this job. Your kids will teach you how to be a parent, and if you're not good at learning, then you're going to be on your way to insane in a little less than a year, unless you're an overachiever.

When your kid is fighting with you because he wants the Batman cup instead of the Spider-Man cup you just handed him, and there's no Batman cup in your pantry, you'll take another step toward insane (the argument will last hours). When your kid only wants to wear sweat pants to school and there are no more left in his closet, which means he'll whine for an hour about how you should do laundry right this minute—and this kid is supposed to be the "easy" kid in the mix—you will slip a little farther down the road to insanity. When your kid calls you the best parent ever and then rages, two minutes later, about how you're the worst parent in the history of all parents in the whole world, you'll sidle up to your good friend insanity, slip your arm around his shoulders (yes, insanity is a "he"), and stay a while.

Trauma

Sometimes, when you've had kids for quite a long time, you'll feel like maybe you've undergone a bit of trauma. You'll see a three-year-old, especially, and start shaking, and you can't quite explain why, until you get back home and remember that your three-year-old twins were pretty much tyrants for a whole year of their lives, and, yeah, it was quite traumatic cleaning up poop smeared on walls every day for forty days and you'd be just fine if you never had to shake hands with another three-year-old for the rest of your life.

(Maybe not the rest of your life. But at least for now, until the trauma subsides.)

Insomnia

Kids aren't great at sleep most of the time. We had a year of no sleep when my twins were three, because they liked to roam the house and destroy things (or attempt to destroy themselves unwittingly). There was no telling what we'd wake up to in the morning. Sometimes we woke up to an entire closet emptied and twelve shirts layered on one boy. Sometimes we woke up to toothpaste paintings on the walls. Sometimes we woke up to the entire contents of a vitamin bottle (a child-proofed one, of course) consumed.

We finally got smart and installed a doorknob backwards so we could lock them in their room and save them from themselves.

Vomiting

Maybe I just have a weak stomach, but there are some terrible smells my sons emit that make me gag and almost vomit. Boys are skilled at collecting feces, which means they hardly ever flush the toilet, which means my house smells like a swamp, and it has nothing to do with a sewage backup—well, at least not in the pipes. Sometimes I'm even fortunate enough to get a present from them in *my* bathroom, which is supposed to be off-limits to any male younger than age thirty.

I've also been close to vomiting over some of the things my sons say, the way they chew on the bottoms of their shoes after walking the downtown streets of my city (they say it "tastes good."), when their SBDs (Silent But Deadlies—a noxious gas released from the sphincter), singe my nose hairs. I want to vomit when they stick their tongue all the way up to their nose to "wipe the snot" off their upper lip.

I'll stop now. I feel a little sick.

Paralysis

Kids cause paralysis by invoking parental fear. This typically happens when my sons are trying to slide down the stairs face first and I know—I just know—this will be the end of someone. They'll cause parental paralysis when they're trying to slip down that playground fire station pole so they can run from their daddy while playing tag, even though the top of the pole is six feet off the ground and they're barely four feet tall. They cause it when they think they can cross a street on their own and there's a car coming with a driver in it who isn't paying attention. Which is exactly why we invested in child leashes for our know-it-all twins.

Night terrors

Kids will cause night terrors if or when you wake up in the middle of the night and there's the face of a child, illuminated by the glow of the moon but otherwise obscured in darkness, staring at you, looking like this time he might not just take your brain but also your soul. They'll cause night terrors when you hear their footsteps at three in the morning and you know it's the wanderers wandering, looking for something to destroy. They'll cause night terrors when your alarm clangs and your first thought is what will you possibly fix for breakfast when your refrigerator was emptied by the bottomless pit (or several of them) yesterday.

Hallucinations

Hallucinations are not formally a side effect of children but a side side effect. Hallucinations are really caused by lack of sleep, which is caused by children. Sometimes you'll wake in the middle of the night and think there's a creepy kid standing at the side of your bed, but there isn't. Sometimes you'll see a kid coming at you, and you'll prepare yourself, stiffening in some places, loosening in others, but the impact never comes because you saw something that wasn't really there. Sometimes you see an extra twin, when one is really hiding so he can use those scissors his older brother left out to cut up the pages of the most expensive library book you have in your house.

Side effect labels would be nice, wouldn't they? Then again, no one would likely voluntarily have kids if they came with all the side effects labels a parent would need. So maybe it's actually better to choose surprise rather than awareness.

Because the light kids blaze into a life is worth every one of these side effects.

Even the night terrors.

Don't miss out on a Crash Test Parents release! Visit www.crashtestparents.com to keep up-to-date on book and product releases and to access bonus material.

Appendix A: Pros and Cons to Consider in the Parenting Life

Letting a three-year-old pick out his own clothes
Pro: You don't actually have to do any work.
Con: The whole closet ends up on the floor.

Making kids wash the dishes
Pro: You get a break.
Con: The counter becomes a swimming pool.

Letting your kids' friends come over
Pro: They're entertained.
Con: There are a billion kids in the house, asking for things.

Having pizza for dinner
Pro: Nobody complains about what's for dinner.
Con: The house smells like a sulfur plant.

Having a family movie night
Pro: You don't have to hear any words for two hours.
Con: They're still bouncing off the walls an hour later.

Giving kids dessert
Pro: They'll love your forever (which is not as long as it sounds).
Con: You'll learn that there actually *is* such a thing as bouncing off the walls.

Taking your kids to a birthday party
Pro: They're entertained for three hours.
Con: They have to come home.

Letting your toddler watch an episode of "Super Why"
Pro: He's learning letters.
Con: That theme song will be stuck in your head all day.

Letting a three-year-old drink from a big boy cup
Pro: You'll make his day.
Con: You'll be cleaning up on aisle kitchen all day.

Leaving your kid home alone
Pro: No more sitters!
Con: No more food in the fridge!

Walking to school with your kids
Pro: You get a little exercise.
Con: You've never heard so many words in your life.

Letting your kids take a day off from chores
Pro: You'll get them done faster.

Con: They'll forget the last two thousand days of doing chores in favor of this one day off.

Making kids put their own laundry away
Pro: YOU DON'T HAVE TO DO IT!
Con: They'll look like a piece of used tissue paper. Every day.

Teaching your kid how to arm fart
Pro: Entertainment. For hours.
Con: You have to listen to it.

Taking your kids to the children's museum
Pro: They'll have so much fun.
Con: They'll have so much fun you'll have to drag them out the door.

Letting kids help in the kitchen
Pro: Maybe, with enough practice, you won't always have to cook.
Con: The kitchen looks like a crime scene.

Running a creative house
Pro: The kids create something amazing every day.
Con: You'll end up with science projects in your freezer. Or the toilet.

Appendix B: True Confessions of a Real Parent

When your kid inhales five green apples while you're folding laundry and you want to say, "I hope you like having diarrhea." But you know he probably would.

When you kid says "I hate you," and you want to say, yeah, well, I don't really like you all that much right now, either.

When your kid says he wants to run away and you want to say, "Here's a sandwich. Make it last. Practice rationing."

When your kid says, "I don't like that," before he's tasted dinner and you want to say, "Then you get a big bowl of nunya for dinner. And it's delicious."

When your kid gets hit by his brother and you want to say, "Yeah, you deserved that."

When your kid won't stop copying you and you want to Duct tape his mouth shut.

When your kid asks, "Are we almost there?" before you're even out of the neighborhood and you want to turn the car back around, park it in your driveway and say, "Yep. We are now."

When your kids won't stop arguing and you want to join in on the slap fight that breaks out amongst them.

When your kid tells you that you still look pregnant, are

we having another baby? and you want to eat the entire package of chocolate instead of just one piece.

When your kid says his friends don't do chores and you're the worst parent ever and you want to do a victory dance in your kitchen because this is your first parenting award.

When your five-year-old says can I PLEASE vacuum and you want to squeal as much as he does when you say yes.

But you don't want to seem too eager.

When someone gives your kid shoes with laces and he can't tie his shoes yet. And you're running late. And they're the only shoes he wants to wear. And you want to destroy them.

When your kid was actually listening for once and you said something you probably shouldn't have.

When your kid is whining so hard you want to lock him outside.

When you're vacuuming the floor and you pretend not to see that one LEGO piece. Because there are forty billion more where that one came from.

When your kid calls you greedy for eating the last brownie and you want to remind him about the birthday party he recently had wherein he ate eleven cookies and was sick all night.

When you leave a room for a second and your kid takes the opportunity to dismantle your laptop and you want to dismantle his face.

But you don't. Because you're a good, patient parent with a healthy sense of humor.

About the Author

Rachel is the CCO (Chief Confessions Officer) of the Toalson household, not only expertly skilled in providing her own confessions, strewn about the house in personal journals and woven into essays that print all over the world, but also in ferreting out the confessions of her children. From shifty eyes and splotchy necks to significant or obscure plot holes in explanations and stories, Rachel has heard and seen just about everything. She regularly dons her Sherlock Holmes spectacles and examines evidence in order to get to the bottom of who ate all the green apples (she doesn't usually have to wait long for this one to catch up with the unsuspecting thief), who's responsible for the giant hole in the backyard, and who stole her pen (necessitating this morning's signing of folders in crayon).

When she's not listening to the wild stories of her children or telling them tales of her own, she can often be found rearranging rooms in her house (she prefers minimalism), baking banana bread with old bananas (she hates food waste), and signing endless agendas, reading folders, report cards, and permission slips.

She is the author of the humor essay books *Parenthood: Has Anyone Seen My Sanity?*, *This Life With Boys*, *The Life-*

Changing Madness of Tidying Up After Children, and *Hills I'll Probably Lie Down On*; multiple poetry books; and several stories for kids under the pen names R.L. Toalson and L.R. Patton.

Rachel lives with her husband and six sons in San Antonio, Texas.

Author's Note

My dear reader,

I hope that in the pages of this book you have found enough solidarity to continue living your parenting life with confidence, hope, and joy. It is both a privilege and a challenge to raise children, but it leans much closer to challenge when we are attempting to do it—and to do it *all*—without a community of people around us. Walls appear to keep us safe, but they also keep us isolated in damaging ways. And I hope that you have seen the value of tearing down your walls and telling your parenting stories—whether they are cloaked in humor or they contain all the serious contemplation you could possibly cram into a string of words. It has always been one of my deepest philosophies that we find ourselves in each other. I hope you remember that as you go about your days and years.

Thank you for reading this book and supporting my work. Please consider leaving a review wherever you bought it. Reviews do a number of things; most importantly, they help get books into the hands of other readers.

And if you can think of anyone who needs some laughter in his or her parenting life, please share this book with them. There is nothing more bolstering than recognizing that you and your kids are not so different from other parents and kids.

You'll be breaking down walls, too.
In love,
Rachel

Acknowledgments

With any book like this, when I am poking fun at myself and my family—which, by definition, includes other people—I must first thank my husband and sweet sons for being willing, in my cracking open my life, to have their own lives cracked open. Thank you for your hilarity, for your patience, and for your unending humor. Just the other night one of you said, after sending your daddy and me into a stitch of laughter, "Wow! I can make my parents laugh!" You certainly can. And it makes life glorious.

Thank you to all the editors and publications—too many to name here—that have printed versions of these essays. Thank you for giving my humor a place and proving it was necessary.

Thank you to Erma Bombeck and Shirley Jackson, whose real-life parenting stories I still adore.

And thank you to all my readers, whose "Oh my goodness! Me too!" always gives me the necessary lift I need to carry on.

Crash Test Parents

Enjoy more from the Crash Test Parents series:

www.crashtestparents.com

www.ingramcontent.com/pod-product-compliance
Lightning Source LLC
Chambersburg PA
CBHW030316100526
44592CB00010B/459

Are you a parent who needs a little dose of humor and hope?

For a limited time, pick up your FREE copies of *Guide to Surviving a Year* and *Guide to Self Esteem* and laugh your way back into hope. Or maybe just survival.

Get your FREE copies at:
racheltoalson.com/SurvivingAYear